ALF BLACKBURN'S
WAR MEMOIRS

An ordinary soldier recounts his time
serving in the Desert, Sicily and D-Day
Campaigns of WW2

Jan King   (née Blackburn)

1

Contents

Introduction

This is the story of an ordinary soldier's experiences serving with the Green Howards during World War 2.

Alf Blackburn was my father. As was the case with the majority of men of his generation, he never spoke about his wartime exploits. However, during the late 1960's he did recount his experiences orally, and recorded them onto cassette tapes. He described his initial training and then his active service fighting in the North African Desert Campaign, Sicily and finally Normandy where he was blown up by a mortar bomb.

He explained what life was like, the places he visited and the hardships endured, without going into too much graphic detail about the horrors he must have witnessed. His genuinely modest account, which is funny at times, gives an incredible insight into his war and paints a vivid description of his adventures. Many thousands like him never came home. I have tried to faithfully transcribe his words into this book.

Jan King (Blackburn) July 2022

This book is dedicated to Michael, Christopher and Sarah.
The grandchildren who never got to meet him.

Alfred Blackburn   15.11.1922 – 19.07.1976

The Beginning

In 1939 I was serving my time as an apprentice bricklayer and all building activities were concentrated on the war effort, such as coastal defences and munitions factories. We came under the Emergency Powers Act whereby we could be sent anywhere without any notice whatsoever. At the time I was only 17 years of age and considered rather young to be posted out of the area. I was therefore working locally in County Durham on coastal defences at Seaburn, Roker and Whitburn. We were installing fortifications and emplacements for six inch naval guns, and also searchlight and observation posts along the cliff tops on the Holy Rock. It was interesting work but at the time the German air force was raiding on rather a large scale over the coastal towns of England. It was not unusual for work to be suspended whilst a lone raider was hurriedly chased away from the area. Being very young at the time it was all quite a novelty to me. To be honest I thoroughly enjoyed this break in the monotonous routine but even then I never imagined that I would end up in the armed forces.

Somehow this war wasn't going to last long; everyone was optimistic that it would be over in about six months.

After working on the coastal defences, I was asked to go to an aerodrome at Acklington in Northumberland where we were extending the airport and building a few facilities for the existing fighter base.

It was mid-winter and the weather was atrocious; in fact it was so bad that we had to return home after only one week.

After 'jobbing around' locally for a while I was asked to return to Acklington but declined. Shortly after this I was asked to go into digs in Cumberland, where another government contract was in progress. This involved building houses for the technicians that were moving onto the west coast to supervise defence contracts. I agreed to go and began work on the housing site. I was there for just over six months and really enjoyed the experience of living in digs and meeting new people, all of whom I found very amenable. It was late in 1941 when this contract ended and I returned home, but once again all work was stopped due to severe weather conditions. While in Cumberland I had undergone a medical for the armed forces and it was during this cessation of work in the winter of 1941 that I received my papers to report to Cleethorpes, to join the Worcestershire regiment of the British Army.

In those days people didn't travel far from home, money was very scarce and holidays were unheard of unless you were wealthy. The furthest I had travelled away from home was to Cumberland and I had no idea where the Worcestershire regiment was situated. Homesickness was never an issue with me as in those days we were brought up to be self-reliant and to take the knocks that the times were inclined to bestow upon us.

We left school at age 14 and were expected to take any job that was available, in order that we could begin to contribute to the upkeep of the family. Times were very hard. However, one positive outcome of the war was that it released jobs to a great number of people. Those that were not in the armed forces were once again in full time employment.

Cleethorpes for Training and then Embarkation

On a bitterly cold evening in February 1942 I arrived at Cleethorpes. I was picked up by an officer and a sergeant in a 15 cwt. truck, and taken to a civilian terraced house which was to be my billet. I was given a meal of greasy fried spam and bedded down on the floor of this civilian accommodation. All trainees and staff were billeted in civilian houses with ordinary working people as neighbours. We trained in the back streets and any open spaces that could be found. Here I met a lot of strange speaking people; the majority of the other lads came from Worcestershire and as I was the only Geordie amongst them, they found me quite a novelty. One thing we all had in common was youth and we were all keen. The training was hard and we were subjected to the kind of discipline that we had not experienced previously, but I must admit I thoroughly enjoyed it. The training staff were not too strict; perhaps having civilian neighbours caused them to modify their normal behaviour! On Sunday afternoons our neighbours invited us into their homes for a game of billiards or a bite to eat, overall a very gentle introduction to life in the army.

After this initial training I was posted to Southwold on the Suffolk coast where we were manning heavy Vickers machine guns. We did not know how to fire them, in fact, although we were in charge of ten guns, there was only one person in our group capable of handling them. Whilst doing our guard duty and 'stands at the guns' we tried to learn as much as possible about these complex pieces of machinery and found it all extremely interesting. The weather was fine and our surroundings pleasant so in our free time we sunbathed, but soon our time at Southwold came to an end.

We were sent to Market Rasen and on arrival there I was told to report to the company commander who asked me if I had any objections to being posted abroad on active service. Of course at my young age there were no objections forthcoming. Generally, at that time, everyone wanted to do 'their bit' and I was no exception. We were sent to a holding battalion while the 'powers that be' made the arrangements for our movement, which seemed to take forever. We thought we would never leave! However, after about two weeks of embarkation leave, we were sent to Lincoln and boarded a train to Gourock in Scotland. We journeyed through the night until we came to Durham Station where we were forced to stop because of an on-going air-raid.

During this time we hung out of the train windows watching the ack-ack and the search lights. Being in County Durham and so close to Durham City, I began to feel pangs of homesickness. These feelings worsened as we travelled further north and came to Fence Houses Station, being only a few miles from home. As I gazed out of the window in the moonlight I could see the Britannia Hotel and I thought to myself, "It's going to be a long time before I see this place again".

We arrived in Gourock and embarked on the Largs Bay, the sister ship of the Jarvis Bay, a merchant ship which had been notable in action earlier in the war. We found it fascinating to be on the sister ship of this particular vessel, as it gave us more of an idea what the Jarvis Bay was really like. None of us had been on a boat before and we were a little overawed, especially at its size.

We were so busy drinking in this new experience that we didn't give a thought to our ultimate destination, of which we knew very little. We had been issued with tropical gear but this didn't really tell us anything. We sailed round the northern tip of Ireland into the Atlantic where packs of U-Boats were hanging around. After a few false alarms we pushed out into the Atlantic where we were to see nothing for days on end. Many of us experienced sea sickness for the first time, and our first sighting of land was Freetown on the west coast of Africa. We pulled into Freetown to take on provisions and mail, and to remove any sick that needed attention. After one or two days we proceeded south round the Cape and into the port at Durban, where we disembarked from the ship.

We were then taken to Clairwood Camp, which was just outside of Durban. This was a holding camp; a vast place

10

that was to hold all of the troops passing through Durban on their way to the Middle East, or other theatres of war. We were to be there for six weeks and our stay was very enjoyable. Fresh fruit was in abundance, ice-cream, cigarettes; in fact everything that was rationed at home was easily obtainable. The only thing we were short of was money!

The South African population did not seem overjoyed at our presence and we speculated the Australians who had been there before us had perhaps caused them a few problems.

There was a British settlement in Durban and they were always glad to see anyone from the 'home country'. I had with me the address of an old friend of the family and one Sunday I decided to look him up, as my brother George had done before me. I found his bungalow quite easily, and was made most welcome by both him and his family. They took me for a drive in their car and showed me the places of interest in Durban.

I was amazed at the standard of living enjoyed by the British living there. They had servants to do housework and the gardening, and look after the children. Owning a car was quite the norm, whereas in England at that time cars were very few and far between. Most ordinary working people's budgets would only stretch to a motorbike at best.

Our six week stay in Durban came to an end and we were moved inland to a town called Pietermaritzburg. This was a town inhabited by the white South Africans of Dutch origin, the Boers, and they didn't like the British. We were instructed to be on our best behaviour so as not to antagonise the police. During our stay there we were given an insight into how the black people of South Africa were treated by the Boers. Quite frankly I was disgusted and not at all surprised at the unrest that was to follow in later years, because I had seen at first-hand the way they were treated, and it left an awful lot to be desired.

We were under strict instructions not to interfere in any incident that we might witness, and there were many. After my time in Pietermaritzburg I found that I had developed sympathy for the coloured population, feelings which I had not previously held. I don't think that I could have tolerated the humiliating treatment they were forced to endure.

Two weeks later we returned to Durban and embarked upon a French ship called the Felix-Rouselle. This was not as impressive as the Largs Bay. It was very dirty and the toilet facilities could certainly have been much better! We sailed along the east coast of Africa into the Red Sea and finally arrived at Port Tewfik, where we disembarked and were taken to a holding unit on the Suez strip.

I knew that my brother George was stationed somewhere in the area and intended to look him up, but unfortunately time did not permit. We thought we were going to be there for a few months but this proved not to be the case. In fact we were only held there for a short time as reinforcements for the Eighth Army.

Joining the Green Howards to Train for the Desert

Our camp was positioned at the bottom of some rocky escarpments which were about 250 feet high. As part of our training we had to climb to the top and descend the other side, then find our own way back to camp. This went on day after day, interspersed with foot and arms drill, and ordinary camp duties prior to going 'up the blue', which was our name for the desert at the time.

Before long, we got the order to move and were bundled into trucks and taken north along a coast road which ran from Alexandria to Tunis and beyond. This was the only Tarmacadam road that I ever saw during my stay in Africa and we travelled along it as far as it went. There were branches off onto tracks that were marked by the insignia of various divisions of the Army which were present in the desert at that particular time.

There was the Seventh Armoured, the Fourth Indian Division and the Fiftieth Northumbrian. The latter being the division we would join as part of reinforcements for the Sixth Green Howards. However, joining a regiment from the north whilst being very acceptable to me, was greeted with some dismay from the other lads. They had never heard of the Green Howards or indeed the famous Durham Light Infantry. These regiments were as 'foreign' to them as the Worcesters had been to me. I was secretly rather pleased with the way things had turned out, as I was joining a regiment which perhaps I should have been with from the start.

We were interviewed by the commanding officer (C.O.) of the battalion and assigned to our various companies. I was to join C Company and after a preliminary pep talk was sent to number 13 platoon. Initially my thoughts were, "Oh no not 13, unlucky for some"! However any fears that I may have had regarding the number 13 were subsequently dispelled, as nothing really bad happened whilst I was in this platoon. I even began to regard it as a good luck omen. We were inspected by the company commander who seemed rather surprised that I, being a member of the Worcestershire Regiment, actually came from County Durham.

This was at the time of Alamein and we were reinforcing the Green Howards because of the severe losses they had sustained. We began desert training and were soon to realise how easy our lives had been up to this point. We had not previously experienced any real shortages, but now we were in an active regiment, a fighting unit, and we had to suffer all the hardships that went with desert life at that time; we certainly began to feel the pinch.

Life in the Desert

I would like to tell you more about life in the desert, and although it is difficult to paint a true picture, I will try and portray it as best I can.

Unless engaged in battle we were provided with three meals a day; if we were fighting we had to miss meals as it would have been impossible to get food to us. Our first meal of the day of course was breakfast, and for this we were given tinned bacon, two biscuits, some margarine, half a pint of tea and a ladle of some appalling other stuff. This was made up from biscuit crumbs soaked in water, with a drop of evaporated milk added and made into a sort of porridge. This biscuit mix may have looked revolting but we were very glad to eat it, as this was to be our staple diet henceforth.

We were also given a water bottle containing one pint of drinking water which was to be our ration for the next 24 hours. The temptation to drink during the searing daytime heat was so great but we found that it was much better to leave the water until after sunset when the temperature plummeted. Thus cooling the water down and making it more palatable. However it still seemed to taste of petrol or diesel!

We were also given half a pint of water for washing purposes. Anyone that has ever tried to wash and shave in half a pint of water will understand the difficulties we faced. We decided as a section to pool our water into a five gallon drum and wash in rotation. After we had finished washing, the water was used to wash our underclothes and then, although this may sound pretty revolting, we strained what was left and used it to make some tea!

I think this should give some idea as to how critical the water situation was. The tea was served at breakfast and we were to get nothing more until midday. Then we were given two biscuits, some margarine and jam, all of which came out of tins, and another half pint of tea. There were cooks to prepare an evening meal but it depended on our position as to whether or not we would receive it. All being well the evening meal consisted of beef broth and some tinned rice pudding, and another half pint of tea. This would be the meal we would receive day after day with no variation. On two occasions during my stay in the desert we were given bread, which by the time it reached us was covered in mould. It was only a small loaf to be shared among the whole section, and if this procedure was not carried out accurately there would be dissension in the ranks! Therefore we all kept a watchful eye on the person appointed to divide the bread, just in case he kept a larger portion for himself.

As and when we needed toilet facilities we had to dig our own; away from where the rest of the platoon was positioned. We rarely had time to cover our waste matter because we had no sooner dropped our slacks when swarms of Egyptian dung beetles landed. They did not harm us, just took what we had to offer and departed.

There were also a few varieties of lizards and if we lifted certain rocks we were almost sure to find scorpions. Although they have a dangerous reputation, not one of us ever experienced a sting, even though we were sleeping on the sand.

Flies however were a major problem, and they caused a great deal of discomfort. Each member of the platoon had his own swarm surrounding and pestering him; almost to the point of driving him crazy. They gathered in clusters at every moist orifice available to them; around the eyes, the mouth and the nostrils. If anyone had the slightest wound, even a small scratch, they would eat away at the flesh leaving gaping wounds and scars that had to be seen to be believed. Desert sores could quite easily become the size of half-crowns! The term 'fly happy' was used to describe someone who had 'cracked' owing to the persistence of the flies. They were there from sunup to sundown, and did not leave us alone for one minute. I very quickly learned to cover up even the smallest of scratches, because combined with our poor washing facilities, infection would very quickly follow after the flies had settled on an open sore. Grazes were unavoidable as we were wearing shorts with just a pullover to keep us warm at night.

There were two extremes of temperature; the heat of the day was almost unbearable and at night it was so cold that when we awoke there was a frost covering. When the sun rose it was less than two minutes before we were once again in scorching heat. These rapid changes in temperature took a lot of getting used to.

One of our main everyday concerns was food and water. We never had enough to eat or drink, therefore after any battle if there were any vehicles left around, we would head straight for the radiator to drain off any water before it evaporated. This was life in the desert and it was very hard to bear, particularly so without enough to eat or drink.

Anyone who believed the food parcels sent to the troops actually made it to the frontline was sadly mistaken. We were always short of food, water and cigarettes. The only thing we had plenty of was toothpaste. Whether other units were getting their supplies or not, I don't know, but nothing else seemed to be getting through to us other than toothpaste!

That gives some idea of the hardships we endured just to survive in the desert, without even beginning to contend with the ensuing battles that we were soon to become involved in.

As I said previously we reinforced C Company, the 6th Battalion of the Green Howards, and we moved up into the line. When we took part in a battle we were given the support of Vickers Machine Guns (25 pounders) which were manned by the Cheshire Regiment. They did a marvellous job and I cannot praise them highly enough. They were our firepower and utterly reliable; we did not go into any battle without the support of this heavy machine gun regiment. We were both north-country regiments and seemed to merge as one division. The Cheshire manned 25 pounders rendered a magnificent service.

Anti-tank guns were in a fairly infantile state of development, and seemed to have little effect against the German armour. This was after the so called 'Wakenshaw period', when Adam Wakenshaw was awarded his V.C. for his actions as an anti-tank gunner. It was after Alamein that the anti-tank weapons began to come to the fore and become an effective tool against the German Army.

At the build-up to a battle as many of the 25 pounders as was possible were assembled, and a barrage was laid down to 'soften up' the German position. This was synchronised with the infantry allowing us to advance under the barrage; we moved forward to about 50 yards from the point of impact, then the barrage would lift, enabling us to move further forward until we were right on top of the Germans.

These barrages had to be timed down to the split second, because if they didn't lift at the right time, or we moved too quickly then we could have been caught by our own 'friendly fire'. Indeed there were one or two accidents, but for the most part they did a magnificent job, sometimes firing all night to give us cover.

Prior to commencing battle we would send out patrols to reconnoitre the position of the German troops. I was sent on quite a few of these patrols. We wore woollen pullovers, K.D. shorts (khaki drill), and cap comforters. Cap comforters were a tube of knitted wool, sewn at both ends, and formed into a hat by pushing one end through the tube to the other end. Rolling up the open end produced a cap.

We would only carry the minimum of arms as we were not going to fight but to reconnoitre. We were given a compass bearing and would try to get as close as possible to the German position. Sometimes we were within earshot, providing of course that we successfully negotiated the minefields. The mines planted just below the surface were S-Mines, which were anti-personnel weapons developed by Germany in the 1930s, and used extensively by the German forces. They were small canisters filled with 350 ball bearings and the only thing protruding through the sand were three small prongs, which when stood on, would detonate the powder at the bottom and the canister would explode at about five feet in height. This would scatter the ball bearings at roughly chest height, causing a lot of casualties. They were very effective from the German perspective, and the German forces were very adept at using them. These anti-personnel mines had either 'pull igniters' or 'push igniters' and one trick the Germans had was to place the S-Mines on top of Teller Mines, which were heavy duty anti-tank mines. The pull igniter would be set so that when we tried to dismantle the S-Mine the whole lot would go up.

We had a lot to learn and most of it was learnt the hard way!

Those of us that managed to safely negotiate the landmines pushed on to the German position to assess their firepower and report back. Then our troops would advance under the barrage; the air was thick with smoke, and when it cleared we found ourselves right on top of the German position. Then we began distributing hand grenades as if they were hand-bills or oranges. We didn't throw them; in fact I could never throw a grenade properly! We dropped them in the foxholes where the enemy were taking cover. Those beginning stages of an attack were frenzied and hectic; there was no time to react to the screams or to anyone who had their hands up. In this chaos I am sure that lives were

22

lost unnecessarily, but we were all fighting for our survival. We could not think about being compassionate; only self-preservation because you were fully aware that this day could be your last.

For my first taste of enemy activity I wasn't in the assault company. I was in the reserves bringing up the rear, and in my naivety I felt that I could relax in this position. However I was very much mistaken. We were advancing across some salt flats and kept stopping and starting, and I came across a couple of old boys, Pridmore, and 'Smudger' Smith. Every time we stopped they were digging like hell, and Pridmore turned to me and said, "Hey lad, you'd better dig yourself a hole". I bowed to their experience and began digging with my entrenching tool. It was a beautiful moonlit night and nothing seemed to be happening, so I was fairly relaxed. But I'd only managed a few scoops when I got my first taste of shell fire, an 88 millimetre armour-piercing mortar fire. Our main assault was going in, and of course when that happened, the enemy lets off everything they've got.

I thought that I had experienced fear before, but it was not until this night that I knew what real physical fear was. The mortar bombs were raging, shrapnel was coming down like huge hailstones, and I could hear people being hit with shouts for stretcher bearers. I felt as if the shells were all aimed directly at me! I continued to scoop out sand to make a hole for myself and am not ashamed to admit that I was absolutely petrified. In fact I believe that anyone going through this for the first time who said they were not afraid is a damned liar. I don't believe that I was any more fearful than anyone else; just a normal human being experiencing very normal human emotions, but I was stiff with fear. Most of the lads were in pairs but for some reason I was on my own.

I dug my hole as best I could and said every prayer that I could think of and invented a few others. I had just managed to get most of my body under the sand and was beginning to feel a little safer when a sergeant approached me and told me we were to move forward. "You're kidding aren't you?" I said. At this stage I was still lying flat; but the sergeant told me it would be ok. I know he was just trying to reassure me, but there was no choice in the matter, and we had to just get on with it. I summoned up all of the courage I could muster and rose to my feet petrified, fully expecting to be shot dead as soon as I was standing. This was such a great act of bravery, deserving the V.C. (Victoria Cross) at the very least!

We suffered many casualties during this barrage, the worst I lived through in all of my time in action. It was probably a good thing to go through this at the beginning, as I learnt a lot of lessons that night.

We began advancing forward across the salt flats, stopping periodically, and as soon as we stopped I was digging like a beaver! I must have dug a dozen holes that night; every time we paused, even for ten seconds I was digging like hell. I remember thinking later that the desert must be full of holes dug by me, and no amount of sandstorms would ever fill them in! We continued to advance and came upon a minefield through which the sappers had cleared a gap. They would only sweep a small gap and then lay down a two inch tape as a guide for any troops following. We knew how critical it was to keep to the tape as we could hear the cries of the men that had gone before us and not made it through the minefield. We couldn't see them in the dark; only hear their cries for help. One lad was crying for his mother; it was pitiful to hear his cries in the dark, but we were unable to help as there was no way of reaching him. I presumed and hoped the sappers would eventually make their way to him and also anyone else needing help.

We moved forward and had to clear an area for our assault troops, very soon a skirmish ensued because we had over-run the enemy position. We threw a few grenades around and as the adrenaline kicked in, I found that the knot I had in my stomach caused by fear was beginning to diminish. I told myself that it was the enemy that had caused this situation and got on with the fight in hand. We took the German positions, the shelling subsided, and it became obvious that this battle was at least for the time being, temporarily over. There was no more to be done, other than to dig ourselves in and wait for first light.

Once the sun rose it was imperative that we were dug-in and completely out of sight, because in the desert anything above ground can be seen for miles and miles around. During daylight hours we didn't move about very much, but just sat in our foxholes in the sweltering heat all day. This is why it was preferable to share a foxhole for company, much better to have someone to talk to on those long scorching hot days. We stayed here for a few days to consolidate the position, only moving at dusk, and after these first few days we moved on up towards Mareth.

Mareth would later prove to be a major battle that lasted for eight days. However, before any battle commenced there was a lot of preliminary work to be done, and so we dug-in in front of the strong points. There were usually about three or four of these, in front of the main defensive position. These had to be taken first, and so we dug-in and commenced sending out the 'recce' patrols to find out the enemy's strength and disposition. Then send in the fighting patrols to try and take the position. About four or five of these 'recce' patrols were sent out armed with light automatic weapons and wearing K.D. shorts, pullovers and cap comforters. The latter used instead of tin hats because we had to be as quiet as possible. We went out on compass bearings that had been taken earlier in the day, and weren't intending to engage the enemy. Just trying to get as close as possible in order to ascertain the strength of the strongholds; such as how many machine guns they had, and how many actual troops they had on the ground.

When all the information had been gathered we would report back, before a fighting patrol of 20-25 men would be sent out to take the positions. Around these strong points anti-personnel mines were liberally planted and they caused us a great deal of trouble. I was selected to go with my company to take out one of these strong points. Taking the position didn't present too many problems, but the land mines we encountered on our way out caused a great deal of havoc and we sustained many casualties. We moved onto the strong point and consolidated the position. The other companies had taken their strong points and everything was synchronized ready for the assault on the 'line proper'.

The Germans had dug-in above an escarpment slope and we were below them down on the plain. All the guns they could muster were firing down on us. It was quite a formidable looking obstacle, and indeed it proved to be a much bigger nut to crack than we had first thought it was going to be. Prior to the attack we had dug-in whilst our armour was set up and artillery put in place, ready to lay down the barrage before the assault. As this happened we were taking all of the artillery the enemy could throw at us, and believe me they certainly slammed it down!

In the meantime we once again sent out patrols, probing the line trying to find the whereabouts of the Italian divisions, as we found they were the 'soft underbelly' of any strong point. Therefore it was preferable to begin the assault at that point. Try as we might we had little success in our attempt to find the Italians; we brought prisoners back but they always turned out to be one of the crack German troops, such as the Hermann Goering division or the Panzergrenadiers. We travelled a mile or so along the escarpment but were unable to find any Italians. We continued to dig ourselves in, but things were building up and we knew that it wouldn't be long before the 'attack proper' began.

Sure enough one day we were summoned by Sergeant Docherty who I regarded as a grand old fellow. Although only in his 40's he seemed old to me. We had lost our platoon officer and Docherty was standing in. He was a man we held in high regard, a recipient of the Military Medal and an inspiration to us all. We would often 'take the mickey' out of him, but he always had our best interests at heart, watching over us like a scoutmaster. If he thought we were in any trouble he'd be there to check up on us. When we were under heavy attack from shellfire as soon as there was a lull he'd be there checking up on the troops, and if any had been injured or killed he could not hide his distress. In hindsight I wish we could have let him know just how much he meant to us, but at the time feelings like that were not expressed, nor compliments given.

By the way Sergeant Docherty wasn't killed in action but received orders from the War Department to retire because of his age, at the end of the desert campaign. He was devastated but of course there was nothing he could do about it, and personally I was very sorry to see him go. He came from the same part of County Durham as me and that seemed to give us an extra bond.

Doc sent a message over to our section requesting that Pridmore should go over to see him. Pridmore was a family man, and to me didn't seem to be the fighting type. When he returned we knew from his long face that something serious had happened. The reason for his long face soon became apparent, as Doc had issued him with a sticky bomb to stick on a Tiger Tank.

But there was worse to come as Pridmore told us that Doc wanted to see all of us and when we got there we were each presented with a sticky bomb! He could see from my reaction that I was not too keen on the idea and said to me, "Look lad get over there and stick it on the first bloody tank you see, and blow it to hell".

29

Anyone that has ever seen a Tiger Tank will appreciate how daunting a task this was. The tracks alone were over 2 feet wide, they were an awe inspiring sight and we were going to place puny little sticky bombs on them! To Doc this was all in a day's work.

Advance to Mareth

After receiving the sticky bombs we knew that it wouldn't be long before we were moving into the 'attack proper', and sure enough that night we packed up and began our advance towards Mareth. All along the front of the Mareth line was a huge anti-tank ditch; this was about 12 feet deep, sloping on our side with a sheer bank on the other and a parapet on top. We had to line this parapet and wait for 'zero hour' when it would be time to go over the top.

In the meantime our anti-tank artillery had filled in part of the ditch and were jacking up the anti-tank guns so that they would be able to fire over the top of the parapet. This was an attempt to knock out at least some of the tanks that were lined up on the other side. Our battalion was in the process of moving along the ditch to get into our designated positions when one of our anti-tank guns was hit by a 105 millimetre shell and the explosion threw both gun and crew into the air and they just disappeared in a cloud of smoke. It was very disconcerting to see, but we just had to keep moving to get to our position.

When I arrived at my post I found myself next to a young man by the name of Tommy Long who happened to come from Horden in County Durham. I can only describe him as a miserable young boy who moaned the whole time.

31

He was very depressed and had already said his last prayers, as he thought we had no chance at all. Periodically the German machine guns would sweep the top of the parapet with white tracer. This was a bit off-putting to say the least as it was just over the top of our heads!

Tommy told me to look over the top of the parapet which I duly did, but told him that I could see nothing but a row of dark patches. "Dark patches! What do you think they are, gorse bushes? They're Tigers", Tommy said. Sure enough on further inspection I could see that he was right; the Tigers were all lined up waiting for us and on seeing the massive armour that we had to face I began to feel some of Tommy's despair. Our chances were not looking too favourable, and I felt the sticky bombs that we had been given seemed somewhat inadequate. We might just as well be sticking strawberries on the tanks! Nevertheless these were our orders, and we would soon be given the command to scale the parapet.

We had been sitting there for about half an hour when suddenly Italian grenades started coming over the top of the parapet. These particular grenades were not generally considered to be lethal. They were made of tin which was painted red and had an aluminium cap with a rubber thong. The thong was gripped by the teeth to pull the cap off, and the grenade was thrown. If a direct hit was made then they were capable of inflicting serious bodily harm such as blowing an arm off. However there was very little shrapnel from them, and so there was not much damage done to the surrounding area. They could fall close to you without causing too much harm. The Italians didn't carry anything as lethal as the grenades that we were issued with.

Italian Grenade

Still, they kept coming over and landing in the trench where we were holed up. Presently the battalion C.O. Lieutenant Colonel Lance approached and tapped me on the shoulder saying "Come with me Lad", and with his revolver in hand, promptly jumped over the parapet. Of course I had no option but to follow. On the other side of the parapet was a small patrol of five Italian soldiers who were throwing grenades over the parapet. The Lieutenant shot two of them without a second thought and the other three immediately put their hands up in surrender. I'm not sure that I was of much help as I didn't even fire a shot! I was then instructed to get the prisoners over the parapet to our side so I was prodding them with my bayonet and shepherding them in the right direction. There were a few tense moments before we got back over the parapet because if the machine guns had opened up, I wouldn't have stood a chance with the position I was in.

When we got over to our side of the parapet the Lieutenant said "Right lad, you get these prisoners back to B.H.Q" (Battle Headquarters) and off he went. Tommy said to me "Scarper while you have the chance". I said "Where the Hell is B.H.Q?" "Never mind where it is, just get going, and get out of here while you still can" he said.

So off I went along the ditch prodding the three Italians in front of me not knowing where exactly I was going. Every so often we came upon part of the ditch that had been filled in and there would be a different company on the other side, so I had to shout to let them know that I would be coming over with three Italians. We had to run over the top as every so often there was machine gun fire sweeping across the gaps. It was a bit hairy to say the least. It was quite an ordeal for both myself and the prisoners as everyone wanted to have a bash at them as we proceeded along the trench. They were punched, kicked and hit with rifle butts. One officer in particular seemed as if he would kill one of them, until I intervened, telling him that they were Lieutenant Colonel Lance's prisoners. I was thinking that the sooner I got rid of them the better; they were becoming a liability.

It was not long before I was out of the tank ditch and into a clearing, then all hell broke loose! There was white tracer flying all over the clearing; the Italians dropped face down on the ground and refused to move. I would have liked to have joined them but obviously I couldn't. I shouted and kicked at them like a madman trying to get them up which eventually they did. There was a lot of white tracer flying around and I began to wish I was back in the tank ditch.

Presently a three-tonner truck came into view and there were some radio operators underneath it. I asked them if this was B.H.Q and when they verified that I had found the right place, I informed them I had three prisoners for them. "We don't want them, we don't want them", they voiced anxiously. I replied, "You've got them mate" and I left them. I then walked back through the clearing and into the ditch and headed back to my post.
Tommy Long was surprised to see me back but I told him that it was safer in the ditch, than where I had just been. I asked Tommy what was happening, and he told me that we

were going over the parapet at midnight, so I made ready to go over the top, with my sticky bomb at the ready.

Well, midnight came, then 12.15, and when it got to 12.30 I was wondering if 'zero hour' had been changed. Then along came a Lieutenant Hull who instructed us to get out of there, and believe me, I didn't think it was possible for a ditch to clear as quick as it did. Before I left the ditch I buried the anti-tank grenades that I had been issued with but kept hold of the sticky bomb. We didn't panic but once we cleared the ditch we were off over the salt flats as fast as we could go. I think if no one had stopped us we would have been halfway back to Cairo! We were moving along a track with little semblance of order, not running away, but I would describe it as withdrawing in confusion. It was more like coming out of a football match, rather than an organised retreat, and all of the while the Germans were throwing every shell they had along the track after us. We continued making our way back until we were met by some officers and M.P.'s, who directed us to some open ground where we promptly dug ourselves in, not knowing what was going to happen next.

I was summoned to go over to see Doc and he gave me a tin of self-heating soup to share out with the section. This was something completely new to me and I didn't know what to do with it. About six of us gathered round and I asked what I should do.

One bloke said to take the top off and light the taper at the top and seconds later it would be hot, so I asked someone for a cigarette so as not to show too much light and lit the taper. "What now?" I asked. "Open the tin", I was told, and so in my ignorance I grabbed my bayonet and stabbed the can. Well the whole thing exploded spraying all of us with hot tomato soup! In hindsight I should have put a small hole in the can before lighting the taper. We all got a share of the soup but didn't actually get to taste it, and I was called some rather obscene names! That was the first and last tin of self-heating soup I was to see.

We were still dug-in waiting for orders when we received word the decision had been made that it was impossible to break through the extensive armour that lay in wait along the top of the escarpment; and so the operation had been called off. In the meantime the New Zealanders had been sent south to the end of the escarpment in order to do a flanking movement to position themselves at the rear of the German line thus giving them no alternative but to withdraw.

That was how our battle at Mareth ended; we didn't make a major assault on the line, only the outposts we had taken out earlier.

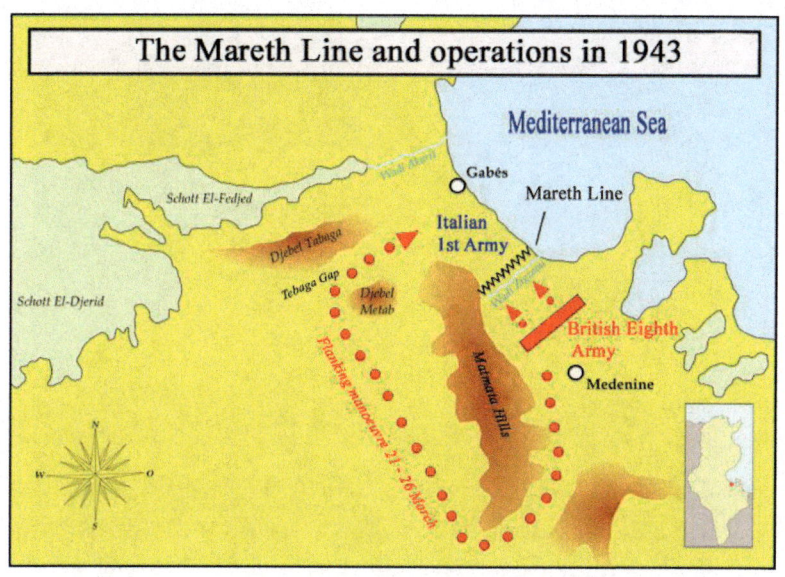

(History of war.org)

British Troops in an anti-tank ditch
(Wikipedia)

We were camped at Regina (also known as Ar Rajmah) in the Cyrenaica area waiting for our next orders. While we were waiting we organised games to help pass the time and relieve the monotony. However one day we were given something different to do. We were loafing around in the early afternoon when a truck drove up and dumped a 45 gallon drum into our company area and half-filled it with water. We gathered around the drum wondering what it was for and were told that it was company bath day! After a few minutes of standing around looking at this half-filled drum of water we began to discuss who was to go first. There was no room for modesty in these circumstances so I volunteered to go first and amidst many cheers I dropped my slacks and promptly jumped into the 45 gallon drum. We certainly had fun that day but by the time we'd all had a bath, the water was fit to plant shrubs in!

We were just beginning to relax when word came through that we were moving back up the desert to rejoin the line. Immediately the tension began to mount, although it had never completely left us, and evidence of these nerves were obvious at times. There only had to be a sudden noise, even something as trivial as shaking a groundsheet and we would all hit the deck.

So we packed up the Company area and jumped on the trucks to catch up with the rest of the Army, who were already a few hundred miles ahead of us. Distances involved during the desert campaign were tremendous so when we boarded the transport we knew that we had quite a journey.

The Battle for Wadi Akarit

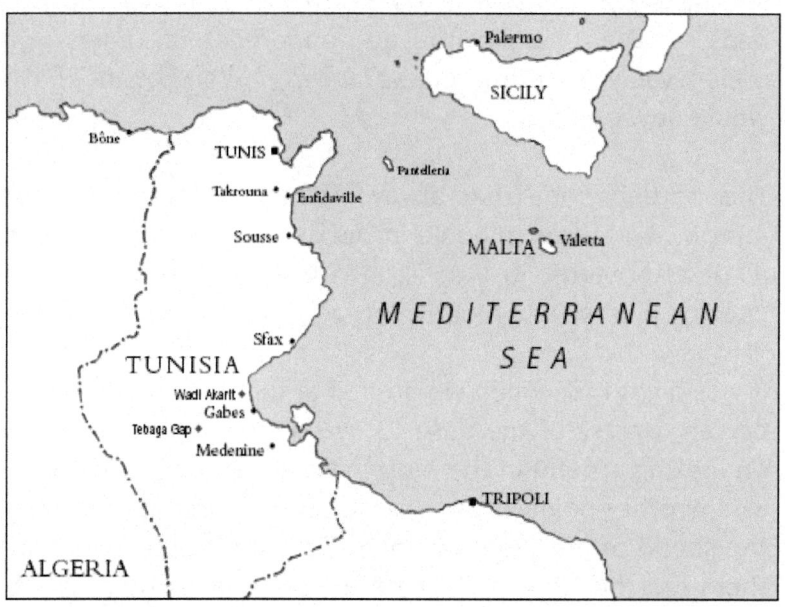

We drove out of Cyrenaica and headed towards Tripolitania and our next mission was to be the battle for Tripoli. After that we stopped just south of a place that was to be our next battle, the Battle of Wadi Akarit. There were quite a few of these wadis, which were in fact just dried up river beds. We had journeyed hundreds of miles, yet unbelievably were still in the desert. We thought that it would never end.

This battle is one that always remains uppermost in my mind when I recall my time in the desert. Everything before it, or afterwards, just pales into insignificance. It was to become a fierce and bloody battle.

It was night time when we arrived at our position in the hot, barren, wastes of the desert. We dug-in for the night and on looking around in the morning it appeared just the same as any other point in the desert. Early afternoon we heard the sound of our planes coming from the south. We heard them first but in the clear desert skies they could also be seen from miles away. They were unmistakably Boston Bombers, easily identified by the high tail fin. We were never overjoyed to see these planes as they were always somewhat erratic in their bombing and immediately we got our heads down as we knew what to expect.

When they were over our divisional lines the Germans opened up with their ack-ack guns. As soon as they were fired on the bomb doors of the planes opened and down came the lot. Our divisional lines were hammered along with the Germans. Whether it was our air force or the Americans there didn't seem to be any liaison with the ground troops, as this happened time and time again. The Bostons came and went, and nothing much more was happening at that moment, but hopefully the Bostons had softened up the position that we would be fighting for in the very near future.

For the moment we had to sit tight awaiting the build-up for the forthcoming battle, and as it happened, a couple of days passed before everything was teed up in readiness to take the enemy position. It was reassuring to see that we were accompanied by a heavy weight of armour; the 25 pounders and the rest of the artillery in formation behind us.

We were somewhat surprised to see so much armour as the terrain that we would be covering probably couldn't be negotiated by the heavy artillery, but we were still pleased to see them.

Morning came, dawn of the first light with the deep purple of the desert, the gunfire, the smoke and the smell of the cordite. All the familiar sounds and smells of a first class battle already in progress. Weaving in between the armour we started to make our way across the plain with the German guns firing over the escarpment and raining shells across the plains. The tank crews admired the way we kept

44

walking amongst all the shellfire. Even though we sustained many casualties it was preferable to us to keep moving. We wouldn't want to be in a tank come hell or high water; better on our own two feet than stuck in a tin box! But at least they were safe from small arms fire which we were very vulnerable to.

We headed off towards the bottom of the escarpments and with all the smoke and shell fire banging on around, we knew it was building up to be a first class barney. We made our way to the foot of the escarpment and on reaching this position the tanks veered off, some to the left and some to the right. We moved further up along the side of the escarpment and when we were near to the top, we lay back onto the rock face watching the armour coming over the plain. It was a terrific, awe-inspiring sight, and very heartening for us, to see this massive weight of armour rolling down in the half light, through the smoke and shell fire.

Meanwhile we were still stuck on the side of the escarpment waiting for the tanks to find an opening through to the wadis in order to give us the heavy firepower required to enable the foot patrols to advance. The 25 pounders were too far behind to be able to pick out a specific target; therefore they could only provide a blanket barrage. We'd been there for about an hour when we learnt that some of the heavy armour trying to get through had been bogged down due to the heavy mines that had been strewn along the entrance to the wadi. A couple of them had been hit and it was impossible to either extricate them or get any more armour through; so another couple of tanks were trying to manoeuvre themselves along the top of the escarpment with a view to firing over the top. Whilst this was going on the Germans were ranging with air bursts along the top of the escarpment; knowing we were there, they were trying to pinpoint their range. The air bursts served two purposes, one of which was to accurately pinpoint our position, and the other was to act as an anti-personnel device. During this process of ranging, air bursts were fired very close to the ground, peppering the area with shrapnel, wounding or killing some of us in the process.

In the meantime the tanks were being brought laboriously up the escarpment so that they were very nearly on top of the ridge. The first tank successfully positioned itself so that his turret and gun were over the top and BANG! He received a direct hit and went up like a torch; it was pitiful to see this huge tank taken out so efficiently. The crew had no chance; it was a blazing inferno, and it was shocking to see how easily it caught fire.

The next tank, God bless him, did exactly the same thing. One would have thought that after seeing what happened to the first one he would have hesitated; but no, he moved up until he was on the skyline but got no further than the

46

first tank, when he also received a direct hit. We saw one crew member trying to get out of the turret when flames engulfed the tank and he was left draped over the side. Such an horrific sight and absolutely nothing we could do about it.

After realising that the heavy armour was not going to be able to give us the necessary support, the 'powers that be' decided that we would have to advance into the wadis and attempt to silence these big guns. This was essential before anything else could move at all. We made our preparations for going over the top and then had to sit back and wait for the command.

I was sitting looking across the plain reflecting on the situation we were in and the forthcoming battle. There was often time for thinking whilst waiting for the next move, and there was certainly plenty to think about. My thoughts were interrupted by the arrival of Billy Fallows, a pal of mine, accompanied by a Captain Claude Hull. It soon became evident that they had got their hands on some alcohol, possibly rum, and Billy was certainly the worse for wear. He had decided that he was going to look me up before the forthcoming battle began; he came rolling towards me hurling abuse at all those he passed on the way. Full of liquid courage Billy was shouting at me, trying to persuade me to go over the top to kill a few Germans. I tried to calm him and get him to sit down, telling him that he would get his chance soon enough. He accused me and the others around of being scared; the drink had definitely got the better of him and I couldn't persuade him to sit down. The shells were still firing over the top and landing at the rear of the escarpment. Suddenly he shouted, "I'm on fire, I'm on fire", but I'm afraid that initially we didn't take a whole lot of notice because of his previous drunken rants. It soon became evident that he had been hit in the back by a piece of shrapnel. We couldn't see very much but he was obviously in a lot of pain. However he was still standing so we didn't think that he was too badly injured. Halfway up the escarpment was an armoured car, one of the observational posts for the 25 pound gunners. One member of the observational crew offered to take Billy back down to the company Battle Headquarters (B.H.Q.) for medical attention; so he was bundled onto the half-track and taken away.

We had too much on our minds to give Billy another thought, and we settled down in waiting for the forthcoming attack. We didn't have long to wait because soon the orders came for us to go over the top, and accompanied by Claude Hull waving his revolver, we climbed over the top of the escarpment. Immediately we were under fire and so we spread out, half running and half crouching, expecting to be hit at any moment. There was quite a distance to cover before we were in a position to hit back.

Alec, a Scottish lad, was number one on the gun and I was his number two; it was my job to carry as many magazines as I could to keep the gun fed for Alec. He also stuffed as many magazines in his pockets, down his shirt, basically anywhere he could, and told me to look after myself and not worry about him. It was difficult to keep up with him; he took off with the gun and I remember wondering if he trained on the mountains at home in Scotland as he ran like a hare. He seemed to be in his element. I only had my rifle and bayonet running over this open ground, whilst being shot at, and then we were among them using our rifles and hand grenades. I was never in a position to use my bayonet; I personally found that bullets and grenades were preferable weapons to use.

Alec seemed to be running here, there and everywhere, and I was frantically trying to catch up with him, in case he needed any of the magazines that I was carrying. I passed Claude Hull sitting behind a rock but kept going until we reached the enemy dugouts. They were massive earthworks and we were running about shooting and slinging hand grenades into the dugouts. Meanwhile our platoon officer, Sergeant Docherty, was trying to recall us to get back some order.

In a battle situation such as this we were fighting to survive, but adrenalin takes over and mayhem ensues. For a while everything seemed a bit chaotic but we efficiently overran the position. The prettiest sight of all for us was the four guns that we had successfully taken, completely intact and in tip top condition. They were not 88 millimetre guns as we had previously thought, but French 75's and they were absolutely perfect; we were overjoyed.

Docherty was trying to get us united into some semblance of order but everyone was running around looking for souvenir weapons such as Berettas, Lugers, or Schmeissers. The Beretta, used by the Italians was a small compact hand pistol, akin to a lady's gun. The Luger was another beautiful weapon, capable of firing 11 shots, and a much sought after souvenir. Another was the Schmeisser which was capable of firing our Thompson submachine gun bullets; however the Thompson couldn't fire the Schmeisser's bullets. This I thought was a testament to German ingenuity. Any weapons we picked up were added to our arsenal and utilised when needed.

Maschinenpistole - MP40

The MP 40 (Maschinenpistole 40) was a German submachine gun which had a relatively low rate of fire and recoil. It was often called the "Schmeisser" by the Allies, after the designer Hugo Schmeisser.

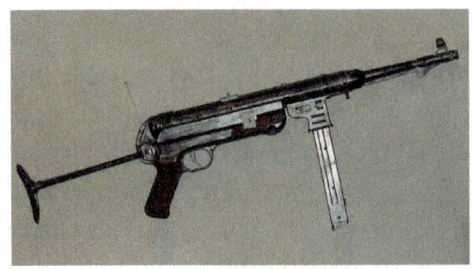

Beretta

Luger

The lads were running about sticking Berettas or Lugers down their shirts. Lance Corporal Till was riding around the wadi on a German motorbike; we were high on adrenalin. Doc was getting angry and shouting the odds but he was cut short as the inevitable happened.

When an enemy position was taken the German troops in the rear already have the range right down to the last foot and immediately started throwing mortars right onto the position. We should have been spreading out, getting ourselves into safer positions.

I was heading down the wadi to join a group of lads, about five or six of them; they were all clustered together at the bottom of the wadi and then BANG, a mortar dropped right in amongst them. Weir, his mate next to him, and another lad were all killed; the corporal, Leonard and Alexander were also wounded. There were usually salvos of six, and so as soon as one stopped we knew the next one was coming. They were dropping in a pattern directly into the wadi, so I dashed for cover into an old foxhole.

After the mortar barrage had finished I emerged from the foxhole, only to be greeted by the pitiful sight of bodies scattered all around. Close to the foxhole in which I had taken refuge, the radio operator was sitting clutching his head. He had been hit in the head and so I went to help him. On closer inspection it didn't seem to be too severe a wound, so I bandaged him up as well as I could and told him to make his way back to B.H.Q. I went over to Weir but he'd had it, Leonard and the others were already being helped.

Overall we were really thrashed. Meanwhile Doc was running around all over the place checking the troops and planning our next move. He grabbed me, gave me a gun, and sent me to a position facing the point from which any counterattack would come from. He asked me how many magazines I had, I told him that I only had three. He said to me, "If you see them coming use those three, then throw the bloody gun at them!" This was a typical Doc statement. He then proceeded to try and organise the rest of the lads.

As it turned out there was only fifteen of us left in the wadi. It wasn't very large and there was good visibility all around. At our rear was a very big hill and every so often there would be a huge thud as an armour piercing shell hit the hill. Once again I felt as if they were aiming directly at me. I was in a good position, facing the guns if any counterattack was forthcoming. I lay behind that gun all afternoon with Doc periodically appearing to check that I was alright. The sun was beating down on my back and sweat was running down my face. I had to keep wiping it from my eyes so that I could see, and all the while I could hear the enemy, Germans or Italians, I wasn't sure which, shouting and revving up the engines of their vehicles just over the escarpment. I could hear the enemy tanks and in all honesty I truly believed that this was the end of the line. I was thinking what little chance we had against the Tiger Tanks.

Presently Doc approached me; he had brought another lad with him to relieve me on the gun, as he wanted me to accompany him. He took me back to the site of the mortar drop because he needed me to confirm the identity of Weir. I knew Weir pretty well; he was a good friend of mine from Manchester. When we got there Weir was sitting propped up on the sand with his knees up as if he was sitting reading a book. He was still wearing his hard hat and small backpack, but his brains were on his cheek. He was covered in dust which seemed to take the starkness out of it somehow. After the identification, Doc instructed me to return to the gun and send the other lad back to him; I returned to my post to resume my stand-to.

Dusk fell and we were still there listening to the continuous shouting of the enemy, and the revving of the tanks. No one came to relieve us, and there was no one to give us covering fire. I remember thinking how hopeless it was. The noise continued until midnight and then things quietened down. Doc was making one of his routine checks and he said to me, "Don't go to sleep". I replied, "Doc there's no bloody danger of me going to sleep!" "It's quiet at the moment" he said, "but keep on your toes". I lay there all night and at first light there wasn't a sound. I asked Doc what was going on. "Well I'm not sure, but I think they've buggered off" he said. Believe me I could have jumped up and kissed him, but he told me to stand-to a little longer until we were sure. Gradually one by one heads were popping up, and then kneeling, until eventually we were all standing and sure enough, much to our amazement, the enemy had retired.

Within half an hour the place was swarming with top brass; there were red hats everywhere. Standing on top of the escarpment they watched the retiring armies through their binoculars. I wondered where on earth they had all come from. It wasn't long before the whole of the Eighth Army passed through us, leaving us to bury our dead and lick our wounds. We had been there, just fifteen of us, and it saddened me to see the rest of the army pass us by as if we didn't matter.

We began clearing up and had something to eat; then the Padre arrived to conduct a service for the dead. We sang 'Abide with Me', and Captain Hull gave a speech, followed by announcing that he had been awarded a Bar to his M.C. for the magnificent job that we'd done that day. That was our reward for the men that we had lost and the position we had taken. I suppose it wasn't in vain, because we did take the guns, and probably saved a lot of carnage in the rear. But I for one will never forget Akarit; every time I think about the desert, Akarit is uppermost in my mind. A memorial was erected on top of the escarpment to the 6th Battalion Green Howards

There was yet another blow to come; I was given the news that Billy didn't make it, and had been buried at the side of the road. This to me was the final straw; I felt like I'd been kicked in the guts. That was my end to Wadi Akarit.

We were reinforced to the left by the 4th Indian Division, advanced through the wadis, and followed in the wake of the rest of the divisions. We headed back to the line, leaving Tripolitania and into the green of Tunisia. It amazed me that one moment we were in the inhospitable desert, and then the scenery gradually softened. Moving forward over a rise I marvelled at the sight of rolling green plains, dotted here and there with white farm houses.

We headed for Medenine with minor skirmishes on the way, including at a place called Wadi Zem Zem, after which we moved up through Homs, on to Gabes, and towards Sfax with more minor skirmishes on route. It was usual for each division to be assigned to a particular battle, and for my division it was Wadi Akarit; after that our job was to give support to the other divisions in their major battles.

There was one more big battle ahead of us; this was when we were pushing the Germans onto Sousse and beyond. We advanced through Sfax to Sousse; the next stop would be Tunis. This was another opportunity for our Commander in Chief, General Montgomery, to give one of his regular eve of battle addresses. I cannot quote him verbatim, but from memory it ended something like this:

> "On my soldiers, on to Tunis, drive the enemy into the sea.
> You and I will see this thing through to the end.
> On to Tunis, drive the enemy into the sea".

We dug in around some olive groves, just north of Sousse with the German Army squeezed into a corner, giving them the sea as their only escape.

The 4th Indian army seemed to be running riot among the Tunisian hills. Alec had re-joined us having recovered from his previous wounding, which turned out to be not of a serious nature.

It was at this time that I met my friend Rennie Shaw. Alec and I were already dug-in under the olive trees, being bitten to death by mosquitos when Rennie and another Yorkshire lad came as our new reinforcements for the section. I found it refreshing to meet someone coming straight out from England, as green behind the ears as they were. Of course, by then, I was a veteran; I'd already been through a lot and knew most of the answers. They asked us why we were sitting in our dugouts and not up in the trees. We said to them, "If you want to get up in the trees go ahead". So off they went and climbed the trees.

They weren't very big trees but they were looking down at us as if thinking we were too thick to have thought of it ourselves. Of course we were sitting back waiting for the shells that were periodically coming over. Sure enough, over they came and the shrapnel was ripping through the olive trees, tearing the leaves off. Down dropped the two lads, faces as white as sheets; Alec and I laughed our heads off and those two lads spent the rest of the afternoon digging frenziedly!

Return to Alexandria

As it turned out this was the end of the line for us; the rest of the divisions had pushed the enemy to the sea and mopped up. We were instructed to gather up our things because we were heading back along the long road to Alexandria for some well-earned leave.

We boarded the transport but this time we were driving back through all of the places with which we had become so familiar; Sousse, Sfax, Gabes, Tripoli, and on to Benghazi. Up the Tokra Pass, through the Derna Pass, Tobruk, Sidi Barrani, Mersa Matruh, El Alamein, and Bob's your uncle, right back to square one.

We thought we were going to get three weeks leave but it turned out to be just three days. I suppose that when a whole army needed leave, logistically three days was all that could be afforded.

When we arrived at base camp, although we bedded down under canvas, there was tremendous excitement at the fact there was a tap with running water. The tap was turned on and we were larking about like school children. After the hardships of the desert, running water was a truly marvellous sight to behold. We enjoyed fresh fruit and I realised how to fully appreciate the simple joys in life.

Before beginning our leave every man in the division had to give a pint of blood. Rennie and I went together; he was in and out really quickly and then it was my turn. My blood did not flow quite so readily and they only managed to take half a pint before I was made to rest before giving the second half. I was surprised at how difficult it was to obtain a pint of blood from me. Rightly or wrongly, I believed it was evidence of how much of a toll my time in the desert had taken on my body.

We enjoyed our leave in Alex and then moved on to Suez to commence training for the operations which were to come in the days and weeks ahead. That was the end of my desert campaign, and as I said earlier, Wadi Akarit always remains uppermost in my mind; I lost many friends there, in particular Billy Fallows.

One always associated battles with the particular friendships formed, and so I look back on the desert campaign with great sadness.

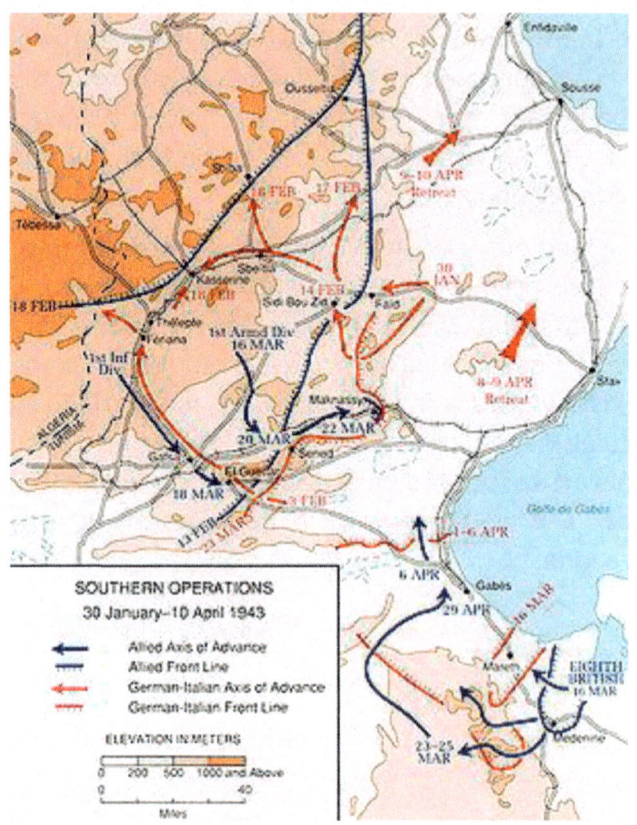

(Map taken from Worldpress.com)

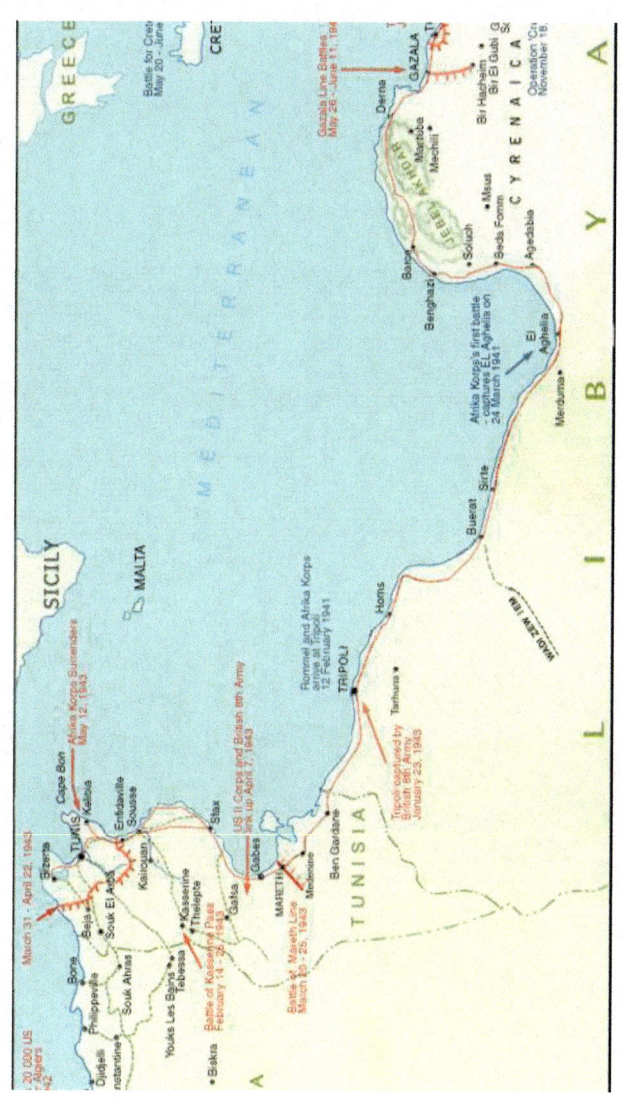

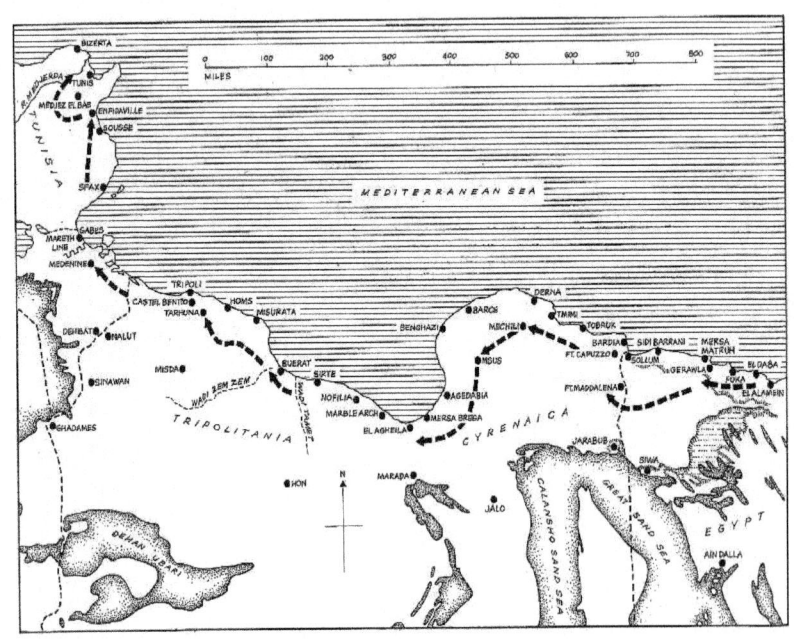

EIGHTH ARMY

Personal Message from the Army Commander

TO BE READ OUT TO ALL TROOPS.

1. Now that the campaign in Africa is finished I want to tell you all, my soldiers, how intensely proud I am of what you have done.

2. Before we began the Battle of Egypt last October I said that together, you and I, we would hit Rommel and his Army "for six" right out of North Africa.

And it has now been done. All those well known enemy Divisions that we have fought, and driven before us over hundreds of miles of African soil from Alamein to Tunis, have now surrendered.

There was no Dunkirk on the beaches of Tunisia; the Royal Navy and the R.A.F. saw to it that the enemy should not get away, and so they were all forced to surrender.

The campaign has ended in a major disaster for the enemy.

3. Your contribution to the complete and final removal of the enemy from Africa has been beyond all praise.

As our Prime Minister said at Tripoli in February last, it will be a great honour to be able to say in years to come:—

"I MARCHED AND FOUGHT WITH THE EIGHTH ARMY."

4. And what of the future? Many of us are probably thinking of our families in the home country, and wondering when we shall be able to see them.

But I would say to you that we can have to-day only one thought, and that is to see this thing through to the end; and then we will be able to return to our families, honourable men.

5. Therefore let us think of the future in this way.

And what ever it may bring to us, I wish each one of you the very best of luck, and good hunting in the battles that are yet to come and which we will fight together.

6. TOGETHER, YOU AND I, WE WILL SEE THIS THING THROUGH TO THE END.

B. L. Montgomery,

TUNISIA, 14th May, 1943.

General, Eighth Army.

Alf with a friend (unknown) in Durban.
Photo from Alf Blackburn's private collection.

Alf Blackburn.
Photo from his private collection.

Alf with his best pal Rennie Shaw.
Photo from Alf's private collection.

Alf with Rennie again. (unknown soldier centre)
Photo from Alf's private collection

Preparation for Sicily

We settled into a routine of training on the flat sands just south of the town of Suez. Every couple of days we would go across the Bitter Lakes and into Sinai for manoeuvres. We were all speculating as to where our next move would be. Some thought perhaps we were going to push on towards Persia, as we were training in the type of terrain that we would experience in that sort of area.

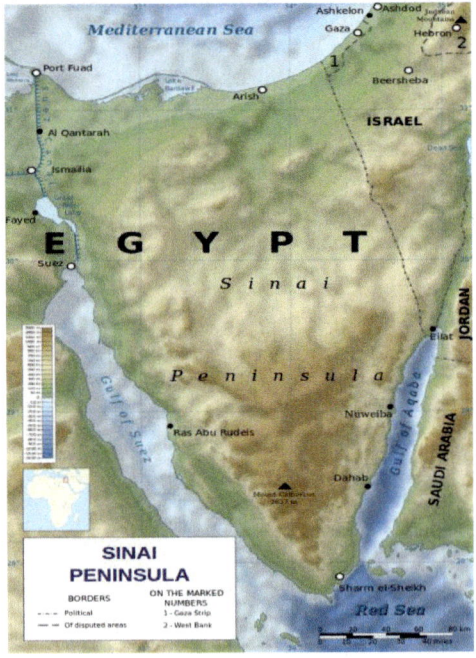

69

No one mentioned England. Even though our desert campaign had ended, we didn't think there was a remote chance of returning home at that stage of the war. The training continued with a new R.S.M. (Regimental Sergeant Major). It soon became evident that he wanted to assert his authority with a clean sweep, as it were.

He put me on three days jankers for smoking on parade, which probably sounds quite reasonable. However, we were all sitting around smoking at the time. He arrived and told us to fall in, at which point I stood up, casually stubbed out the cigarette, and got into line. I happened to be the closest to him at the time, therefore I was singled out. I felt that he was a bit harsh, but obviously I didn't complain; just went to get on with my jankers.

I never found the punishments given out were particularly severe; whilst on active service they were somewhat limited as to what punishments they could mete out. First of all I was sent to the cookhouse after the evening meal to help the cook with any tasks that he required.

During the day I was sent to an area in the camp which looked a bit like a dumping ground, and I was instructed to strip about 50 German S-Mines. I'd had experience of those particular mines in the past, and although the main detonators on the tops had been removed, there were still three more inside which were live, so one couldn't take any chances. One by one I had to strip down all fifty of those mines, first taking the canister to pieces, removing the detonators and gun cotton and putting each to one side. At the bottom of the canister there was a saucer-shaped, lead container filled with gunpowder. This had to be removed and saved in a separate tin; then all of the ball bearings had to be placed in another tin. Not surprisingly, I wasn't interrupted by anyone during this task of work!

One was always wary in case there were any hidden booby traps but somehow this made it rather more exciting. On the whole it was a useful exercise and at the end of it there was nothing I didn't know about those S-Mines. Certainly as a learning experience it was considerably better than reading an instruction manual. The knowledge I gained regarding those mines stayed with me. In fact, to this day I still believe I would be proficient in dismantling one.

There were many things to do after a tour of active duty. Apart from our training, we had to stock up on any stores we needed for the next mission. We had medical checks, more inoculations, and dental treatment such as fillings or extractions. Any kit that needed replacing was also done; I was given a new pair of boots which absolutely crippled me. Getting the correct fitting boots did not seem to be a priority. It wasn't long before those boots became even more of a problem than I had at first anticipated.

The training came to an end and what seemed to me like the whole of the British Army embarked upon a Royal Navy ship. We sailed off into the Med, enjoying the beautiful blue sky and 'life on the ocean wave', still speculating as to our destination. Although the Allies had already attempted an abortive attempt at Greece, we still felt it was one of the possibilities. However this was not to be the case. After a couple of days at sea, the Captain's voice came over the intercom to announce that our destination was the island of Sicily, situated at the toe of Italy. Sicily is a triangular shaped island, only separated from the mainland by a small strip of water.

While aboard ship I was still suffering incredibly due to my ill-fitting boots; I was having so much trouble that I had to report sick and pay a visit to the ship's doctor. It was my first encounter with a Royal Navy doctor and I wasn't too optimistic that he would know that much about feet. However, something had to be done as I knew that I couldn't go on as they were, and I had tried everything possible to make them more comfortable. It was beginning to worry me because once we arrived at our destination; I knew that I would be on my feet 24 hours a day. I thought perhaps I would be issued with some new boots.

However, after the M.O. had spoken to me and checked my feet, his solution was for me to run around barefoot for the remainder of the voyage. Having my doubts regarding the effectiveness of this treatment, I began to wonder if I would be allowed to disembark. I didn't dwell on that idea for too long, thinking that even if my feet had been chopped off, the Army would still have found some way of getting me ashore!

The night before we were due to land I revisited the M.O. for a check-up. He asked me how my feet were and I told him they felt fine. "Put your boots back on, and with a bit of luck you won't have any more bother", he said. To my surprise that proved to be exactly the case, and for some reason that memory has always stayed with me. Reverting to nature is perhaps the best treatment for anyone with serious problems with their feet. And there can be no one more prone to problems with their feet than British Infantrymen on active service!

Landing on Sicily

Our journey soon ended and we landed at Avola, on the south east coast of Sicily. From the ship we were taken ashore on barges and somewhat surprisingly encountered no opposition whatsoever. Therefore we suffered no casualties as we landed.

The same however could not be said of our airborne crews. The gliders were being towed in mostly by American planes. When the ack-ack opened up from over the island they unhitched their gliders, but they were far short of their target and landed in the sea. No one was told for certain what actually happened, but there was a good deal of gossip and bad feeling circulating around the divisions. Whether it was their fault or not I don't know, but the British airborne made it quite clear they didn't want to do any more operations unless they were towed in by British aircraft crews.

On sailing into Avola that morning I could fully understand their sentiments, because the sea was full of the floating bodies of the airborne crew. It appeared the gliders had been released too soon, and the majority had ended up in 'the drink'. The sight of all those bodies floating around in the sea saddened me greatly.

After landing we immediately began climbing up into the hills. Sicily is a very mountainous island with a narrow rocky beach and a few coves. There was a road running around the coast with towns and villages dotted along the way.

The hills were covered with a variety of vegetation; there were vineyards, olives, pears, figs, and oranges. Just about every fruit that you could think of was there as we were climbing. The climb was very hard going; completely different to the terrain of the desert that we had become accustomed to.

Apart from the steep gradient we had to contend with, there was so much overgrown vegetation that it was like a jungle in places.

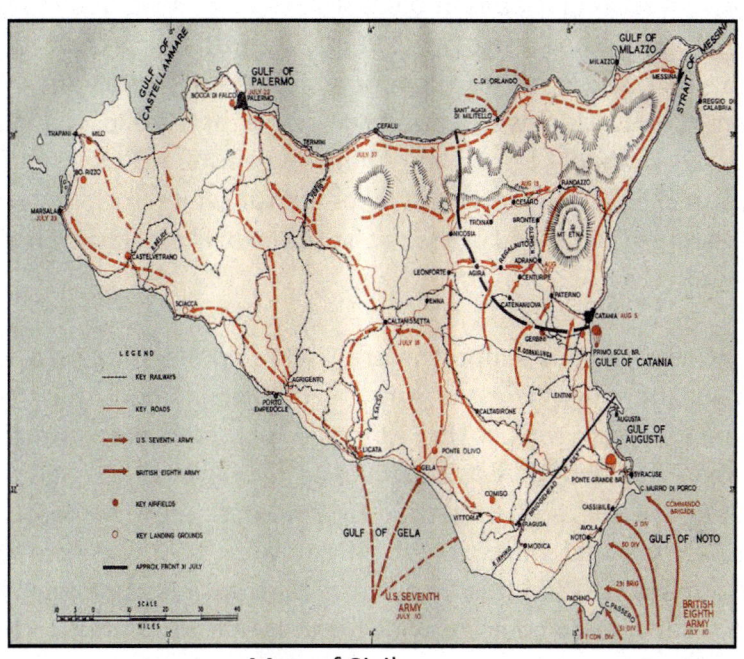

Map of Sicily

After a hard morning's slog, we finally reached the top of the hill and were able to look back over the blue sea of the Mediterranean. It was an incredible sight; the sky and sea were beautiful shades of blue. The sea was absolutely full of our boats; the destroyers, cruisers, and landing craft, with the M.T.B.s (motor torpedo boats) weaving in and out. Far on the horizon were our two heavy battleships banging away; probably firing their shells over Mount Etna. In the centre of it all there was a beautiful white hospital ship bearing a large red cross. It stood out like a jewel in the water.

Periodically, our support aircraft were coming in across the sea; zooming over the top of our heads to attack the enemy's air strips. The air cover provided was effective when available, but as they had to fly in from the mainland of Africa, there was a period of time during the turnaround when we had no cover at all. It wasn't long before the Germans realised this, and timed their assaults upon us and our convoys to coincide with these turnaround times. They had to fly back to Africa, Cyprus or Malta in order to refuel.

Therefore, we only had air cover for about fifty percent of the time, and when we were without air cover we were subjected to an increase in hostile enemy air attacks.
As the enemy fighter bombers took off from the island air strips, there was very little warning of their approach.

They would sneak up the valley in single file formation, usually about five at a time and we weren't aware of them until they were right amongst us. They flew over the top of the hill and zoomed down to bomb our transport convoy on the coast road. There was very little that could be done to stop them, as they flew in low at about house height, and it was virtually impossible to get our Bofor guns and other anti-aircraft weapons down to the trajectory required in order to hit them. Consequently, when we were without our air cover, we really took a pounding. This was to be our main source of worry during the coming days.

If it hadn't been for those air raids, I would have found it difficult to keep my mind on the job in hand. I was that much in awe of the sheer beauty of the island of Sicily, and the things that were growing there. It was a completely new experience for me to be able to simply bend down to pick a tomato or take grapes from the vine.

After the harshness of the desert, we were surrounded by an abundance of new and wonderful things which seemed to be far removed from war. It may sound strange but in spite of all the fighting and battles, whenever I think of Sicily it is the beauty of the place that is uppermost in my mind.
Although our efforts in the Sicilian campaign were by no means negligible, in my opinion it was the Durham Light Infantry that made the most notable contribution.

We were heading up to Messina and on the way were involved in five major battles. One outstanding battle was the battle for Primosole, where once again the Durhams wrote a page for the history books, but more about that later.

We pushed on up the coast carrying all of our gear. This proved to be quite a gruelling task because the road followed the meandering coastline around the hillside which left us very exposed. It was an easy task for the Germans to attack us and in some cases demolish the road completely. This meant that we were obliged to bypass the road and make our way by going into the hills. Transporting our heavy equipment was therefore made even more arduous than it already was. Occasionally we had the use of mules to assist us but most of the time we only had ourselves, the 'two legged mules' to rely upon! It was extremely hard strenuous work from morning to night; in fact it was just a continuous slog, slog, slog.

At this time I was number one on the light machine gun and Rennie was our number two. There had been some changes to our platoon and Docherty, our R.S.M., and all soldiers that had reached a certain age were repatriated back to England. We now had a corporal by the name of Noland, a bad tempered, surly man from Middlesbrough. He was new to us, coming from another platoon, and was very hard to get along with; no one seemed to like him.

I wondered if he had been transferred because of unrest and bad feeling in his previous platoon.

Ted Burton was our platoon commander and we had a Sergeant Errington who was a really nice fellow. I thought he was a 'bit of a toff', and completely the opposite of Docherty, who was a 'rough and ready' sort of a character; although, as I said earlier, we all thought the world of him. Sergeant Errington always showed great concern for the welfare and morale of those serving with him.

Our platoon officer, Ted Burton, was another nice chap; easy to get on with and always ready for a chat when the opportunity arose. However, to be fair, he was a little bit vain and thought that he was the best looking officer in the British army! He was I suppose quite a good looking man, but no one was impressed with looks, good or otherwise, at that stage of the game. One of his jobs was to censor all of our mail and this could be a little bit off-putting, as he delighted in commenting on what we had written. As a consequence, we were somewhat guarded when writing our letters, concerned that they would be read out aloud for the whole section to hear. No one took offence at this; it was all part of the normal banter and camaraderie experienced when part of a close unit, and as I said, he was very well liked. Occasional light heartedness was needed in active service to relieve some of the pressures we had to contend with. We had lost so many officers in the desert campaign that I teased our platoon officer, telling him that he wouldn't last five minutes; not a very reassuring thing to say, but this was the type of banter that went on.

It was only Noland that didn't join in with the light hearted banter, as he always seemed to be in a bad mood. He didn't bother Rennie or me because soon after his arrival we had a showdown with him; making it plain that shouting abuse was not going to gain respect from us or get the best out of the men.

We continued to push on and at times I found the hard physical exercise satisfying, but after so many miles we were all exhausted. I was carrying the light machine gun and Rennie had the magazines, with sweat running off us as we slogged up the hillside which was about a 1 in 4 gradient. I offered to help Rennie with the magazines, as they were a terrific weight, but he was happy to carry on. I thought Rennie had the worst job as although the gun was heavy, it was easier to manoeuvre into a more comfortable position to carry. Then something happened that I'll never forget.

We were slogging along this steep track when Noland appeared in front of us. "That's it!" he said. "That's it; I'm not going another step!" Whereupon he promptly sat down refusing to move; and this don't forget was our section corporal! I was standing next to him so tried to persuade him to get up, telling him that he would be in big trouble.

My pleas were to no avail. "They can all go to hell", he said. "I'm not moving another step." Ted Burton came over to try and ascertain the cause of the commotion. He also tried, without success, to cajole him back to his feet.

Talk about "Sam pick up thy musket"! Anyway Noland was having none of it and still refused to get up. I know it was hard going and we were really stretched to our limit, but Noland was slightly better off than the rest of us because he had less to carry.

Presently the C.O. and the sergeant major arrived and they also tried to persuade him to get up; but also to no avail. The sergeant major said "Right, take his gun away from him", and he put him on open arrest. We took his Thompson machine gun and all his magazines; the gun was given to some other poor lad, and the ammunition was divided up between the rest of the unit. Needless to say, we were not happy at the prospect of not only carrying our own equipment but also Noland's as well. Believe you me, that man was called some really choice names that day, which I won't repeat here!

On reflection, I thought it was the wrong thing to do; it would have been more fitting to hang another gun round his neck. Instead, he was more or less in 'shirt sleeve order' while the rest of the unit were weighted down.

We continued our advance up the track and Noland had to endure a barrage of abuse from the men, who were understandably annoyed. As Rennie and I were already carrying our full whack we were okay because we were not given any extra to carry.

We were heading for Sortino in the province of Syracuse, where we were to mount an attack. As we approached Sortino we could see a deep valley surrounded by rising hills. The Cheshires were already lined up along the high side of the valley, as this was to be the point from where we would begin our attack. Their ammunition was stacked up ready to go, and due to the lack of barrage fire, we would be relying on the heavy machine guns that they had struggled to carry to the top of the hillside. On reaching the top we dropped onto the deck for some long awaited and much needed rest.

We had no idea what lay ahead. There were no patrols to gather information from about the opposition. We had to advance into the unknown, underneath the heavy machine gun fire. This was to be Rennie's first attack and I tried to reassure him, telling him that there would be at least 20 heavy machine guns firing over us. I also told him to keep his head down!

The order was given to stand-to and the decision was made to keep the Bren guns in our section all together, which I must admit I found to be a little foolish. As being grouped together meant that if one got hit, then so would the rest, and bang would go all of our firepower. But of course we had to follow the order to the letter.

Along with Rennie, Ted Burton, and myself there was another young chap in our section; a staunch Welshman who went by the name of Toby. He was a lance corporal and on his arm there was a large snake and a dagger, with the words DEATH BEFORE DISHONOUR. This amused me immensely and I used to tease him about it, although I knew that it was all to do with his Welsh pride. He was a likable chap and very easy to get on with. We stood in darkness, at the ready, preparing to advance down the valley under the fire of our heavy machine guns. I said to Rennie, "Don't panic because in a minute these guns will go off and all hell will break loose; the noise will be terrific but don't worry they are our own guns." Ted Burton had never experienced it and neither had Rennie; I knew how scary it would sound for them and so I was quite prepared for what happened next. I was listening to the sergeant in charge of the guns, because as soon as he gave the order, they would all open up together.

The order was given and the guns began to fire. Unless you've experienced it, the noise of about 20 Vickers machine guns going off over your head is hard to imagine, and almost impossible to describe. Ted Burton hit the deck and Rennie was about to follow, until I grabbed him by the arm saying "I told you what would happen." Ted was lying face down and I was struggling to speak with laughter. "What are you doing down there?" I said rather sheepishly, as he was an officer. Ted Burton rose to his feet. "Phew, that frightened the life out of me", he said. Still laughing I said, "We haven't started fighting yet. Those are our guns!"

I was enjoying myself by teasing them but we quickly had to get back to the job in hand that we were there for. After about 10-15 minutes of solid fire, we were given the order to advance. Keeping below the level of bullets from our machine guns was not difficult to do, because the slope into the valley was quite steep, and as the guns had such a terrific range, we were initially in no danger of being hit.

The guns continued to pour lead into the German positions as we made our way down the steep grassy slope. Slowly at first, then the pace quickened a little, and then increasing to a trot before finally we were running like the clappers. And don't forget, all of this was undertaken in total darkness!

As I said, our three guns were together; Toby and I were side by side with Rennie at the rear. Toby started to speed up down the slope shouting in Welsh as he went, working himself up into a right frenzy with shouting that sounded to me like some ancient Welsh battle cries!

We eventually reached our position and as far as I could see there was nothing to shoot at. We were ordered to dig in and settle down until morning. At first light we looked around but there was nothing to be seen except for one dead German lying in the grass a few hundred yards away.

Word arrived that our commanding officer had been shot in the leg, and that along with the dead German, was the only casualty of that particular battle. No one knew who had shot either but I could state with complete confidence that I was not responsible for shooting the C.O. as I had not fired my gun at all. Toby was amazed that I had been through all of that without firing, and was still in possession of a full magazine.

At the end of every battle we had to strip down our weapons, and clean them ready for inspection, but as mine had not been fired I was spared that particular chore, much to the annoyance of Toby.

On that occasion I couldn't see anything to shoot at and didn't see the point of firing at nothing. I restarted my gentle teasing of Toby mentioning his battle cries, but he never did tell me what he was actually shouting. That was our first battle on the island of Sicily and when it was over, we moved into the orange groves and dug in.

This was a beautiful area with farmhouses scattered around, and terraced vineyards cut into the hillside. Huge figs were drying in the sunshine on boards next to the cottages. It was here that we would have our first encounter with the local Sicilian people; an encounter which saddened us on seeing the abject poverty that these people were enduring.

At this time our food was delivered in boxes known as K-Rations, which were introduced by the Americans when they came into the war. As far as we were concerned we had never had it so good, because the K-Rations not only supplied us with meals. But also cigarettes, chocolate, boiled sweets and tinned puddings, all of which we gratefully received.

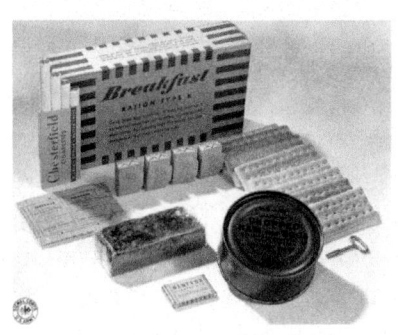

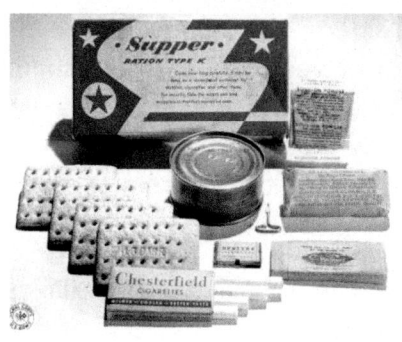

We were settled in the orange grove preparing to tuck into our K-Rations when gradually from behind the trees, children slowly began to appear. They said nothing but stood about 6 yards away from us, quietly watching. They weren't begging but it was obvious to us they were starving. They were dressed like urchins with bare feet and ragged clothes, and of course once we'd seen them, there was no way that we could eat our food, no matter how much we had been looking forward to it.

Gradually with a lot of coaxing we managed to persuade them to approach and very politely they took some chocolate from us. I say us, but in fact they approached everyone in the section apart from me, and for a while I was at a loss as to why this was. Then I realised it was not so much me, but the gun that they were scared of. The large machine gun was always at my side on its tripod and no amount of coaxing could persuade them to come anywhere near me. I found this quite upsetting but the only way that I was personally able to give anything to the children was to move away from the gun, and this went against all of our training. If I bent down just to move the gun, they would scatter in fear. The rifles did not seem to have the same effect.

We continued to advance, relieving many villages on route, and the heavy gun I was carrying proved to be a handicap in more ways than one.

Every time we passed through a village or township, the people greeted us with bottles of wine and garlands of flowers. The women and children would pass me by because of the gun, and then mobbed the rest of the section showering them with the flowers, wine and kisses. It was only the old men of the village that showed no fear of the gun. I did on occasion, try to get someone else to carry the gun but no one would oblige, so I was stuck with it and not too happy about it. I was getting a bit sick of kissing old men, and it would have made a pleasant change to have experienced something more to my taste!

Our lines of advance through the villages were often mined by the Germans making our lives even more hazardous. As we approached one village we saw one villager's chair outside his cottage. On looking closer we could see that he had placed his chair directly over one of the German mines. Then we saw the rest of the street; all the villagers had marked the position of every mine so that we could safely pass. I found this very touching and gratifying to know that the Sicilian people had confidence in us. On passing the old boy sitting outside his cottage, we showered him with sweets and chocolate and left him smiling and looking very pleased with himself.

We continued advancing along the coast road taking turns at being point section. I clearly remember one morning when Rennie and I were leading the platoon, or rather the whole company. We were probing forward and as I had the gun, I was at the front with Rennie by my side. We had been instructed there was a river ahead and our initial aim was to reach the river and reconnoitre the area. At every bend we came to, we stopped, anticipating sighting the river, which we thought would have a bridge with the enemy defending it. On one occasion after stopping, we turned to look behind us and were amazed at the sight that greeted us.

We could see for miles down the long coast road and I'm sure we could see the whole Army behind us including all of our transport vehicles. It suddenly dawned on us the 'power' that we had over our own oncoming troops; because every time we stopped, then of course everyone else had to stop as well. Therefore we decided to stop every now and then, even when it was unnecessary, just for a bit of fun! It might have been a bit of a silly thing to do looking back but it helped us to relieve the monotony of the march. Although of course we still had to remain alert, as we never knew what was around the next bend.

On approaching one such bend we heard someone whistling and singing. We waited nervously but it turned out to be a Sicilian carrying a basket of peaches and appearing not to have a care in the world. We were obliged to stop and search him, during which time he was chatting away constantly, but of course we couldn't understand a word that he said.

We tried to get some information from him; asking about Tedeschi, which was their word for the Germans. "Tedeschi finite" was all we could understand. As far as he was concerned the war was over. It did occur to me that he was of an age that one would expect him to be in the armed forces. I wondered if he had deserted because it was well known that the Italian soldiers were becoming more and more demoralised, and many were surrendering where and whenever they could. After searching his basket we allowed him to continue on his way, but first he gave Rennie and me two of his peaches. They were delicious and I'm sure he didn't get far down the line before his basket became empty! It was heartening to hear from the young Sicilian that the Germans were nowhere in the near vicinity, so as we approached the next bend we were feeling slightly more relaxed.

On the other side of the bend, we found the river we had been looking for but it turned out to be a dry river bed, a common occurrence in the area. We crossed over the river bed and proceeded up the coast road with our transport following along behind. We moved up the hillside and dug in, among what looked like lava rocks. They were very rough and black, and I thought they were probably volcanic; bearing in mind we were not too far away from Etna.

As we seemed to have a quiet moment, Rennie and I decided to tidy ourselves up by having a quick wash and shave. Down the road in the valley our transport was also pulling in for the night, along with the light machine gun carriers that accompanied us on minor sorties.

Rennie and I were halfway through our shave when suddenly over the top of the hill down came the Messerschmitts and the fighter bombers. Some of which had already discarded their bombs so they would strafe us with cannon fire. They flew down in single file strafing along the middle of the road, knocking hell out of our transport and shooting up the carriers. Rennie and I were in a good position to observe all of this. However, things quickly took a turn for the worse when over the hill appeared a fifth plane and this was carrying a massive bomb. It looked massive to us because it was flying so low, and appeared to be just over our heads. As he zoomed down towards the convoy this huge bomb was detached. We were presented with a very eerie sight, as this huge, vicious-looking, black bomb on being released seemed to be hanging in the air, nose pointing downwards. It appeared to be aimed directly between our eyes.

Rennie and I looked at the bomb, and then we looked at each other and together dived under some rocks terrified. We held our breath dreading the impact, convinced that it was about to land right on top of our toecaps!

As it happened it passed safely over us and landed right in the middle of our carriers that were on the road at the bottom of the valley below us. The carnage that followed was almost indescribable. We were covered in debris and rubble that the bomb threw up as it exploded. We knew there wasn't another bomb to come because that was the last aircraft, so we looked around to see what damage had been done. What a terrific mess it had caused; five carriers had been hit and some were completely gone, along with many lives.

An inquiry was later held to establish why the carriers were in such a vulnerable position. The enemy aircraft found them absolutely wide-open and exposed. It was impossible to get the trajectory of the Bofors down quick enough to fire at the planes, as they were flying so close to the ground.

Rennie and I stood up and tried to finish our shave; it was difficult as we were shaking so much. We contemplated as to how fortunate we had been. If our position had been just a little further down on the road then the outcome would have been completely different. Still, that would have been the price of war.

We rested overnight and the following morning we moved out heading towards Lentini, which would be the site of our next skirmish. In my opinion this, and following battles, did not have the same severity as the desert.

Don't get me wrong; we were still in danger of being shot and killed, and if the Germans entered into any battle, they put everything into it. Believe me we still had our hands full, as it were, but to me there was no comparison to the desert battles.

The Germans' main concern was to hold us up while they pulled out as many of their troops over the Messina Strait as was possible. They were beginning their retreat from the island and only fighting selected battles as and when the need arose to slow us down.

Onwards to Lentini

We pressed on to Lentini and after one or two skirmishes, successfully secured it and dug in on the outskirts. On reflection, my attitude to the battles we had in this country must have been influenced by the sheer beauty of the place. We had the sea to our right with mountains and rolling hills to both the left and ahead of us. There were isolated villages scattered here and there, some on top of these hills which appeared almost inaccessible. All along our line of advance we never lost sight of the sea, and at one stage found ourselves walking along the cliff edge with amazing views below. One such view was at Taormina with its blue lagoons and incredibly clear water surrounded by rocks. Apparently this was a favourite holiday destination for the wealthy of the time, and I could certainly see why.

It was impossible to not be affected by such beauty. It was in total conflict with the job that we were there to do. I was in charge of the section because the corporal that had caused us the problems earlier had been moved; mainly due to the fact that he had lost all credibility and respect from the men.

I didn't mind being in charge as my role wasn't really altered. I was still on the gun, and we were all pals; all in it together. It was always the case that the person we looked to for leadership was the one with the most experience, which at this time happened to be me. Whilst dug in for the night we would try to get as much rest as possible, taking our turn to be on guard. It was difficult countryside for guard duty because in the dark, every bush, peach or olive tree, looked like a person moving in the darkness.

At the time we had a young lad from Hartlepool going by the name of Totty assigned to our unit. I'm afraid he was somewhat lacking in common sense and I wondered how he'd managed to get to us. I rather assumed he'd been rejected from every other unit in the British Army before finally being sent to us. Still, he was here and had to take his turn on lookout along with everyone else.

To enable each person to get to the lookout post and back again in the dark, we had a long piece of white tape going from one position to the other. This we held on to and used as a guide, and if someone returned displaying a sense of urgency, we would all stand to.

It was Totty's turn for lookout duty, and I was just dozing off when suddenly he appeared running like hell shouting, "They're coming, they're coming!" Within seconds the whole platoon was standing to. It turned out to be a false alarm and there was absolutely nothing there, not a thing. This started to become a regular occurrence on Totty's watch, and after a few false alarms, I went to Ted Burton and told him that he would have to get rid of him as he was more of a liability than an asset. He had everyone on edge and the men just couldn't rely on him.

So they moved Totty out, where to I did not know, but I hoped he was ok. He was a decent lad just not cut out for the job we had to do. Personally, I thought he would have been better off in the Pioneer Corps or something similar. He definitely didn't belong with us; I'm not saying that the rest of us had the highest intellect but at least we had the necessary acumen needed to survive in the environment we were in.

Every morning at first light we would stand up and look over the valley; it was usually misty first thing and cleared once the sun came up. It was the morning after Totty's departure and we were standing waiting for the mist to clear. Then suddenly just as it was beginning to clear we could see two helmets bobbing about in the distance, but were unable to identify them as they were just too far away. Although we could only see two people, we couldn't be certain until they got nearer, so our best course of action was to lie 'doggo' with weapons at the ready. I got down behind the gun and dropped the sights to zero and lined in on them. They were making quite a bit of noise as they advanced, coming closer and closer through the mist. We could now see their heads and shoulders above the mist and my finger was taught on the trigger. Everyone was teed up ready for action and there were only a few yards in it before they would have got the full firepower of the section down on them.

At the last split second someone shouted, "They're two of our fellows." Believe you me; they were the two luckiest men on the island at that moment, because in two more yards they would have copped the lot.

Looking through the sight of the gun it was impossible for me to distinguish their nationality, and the obvious assumption on seeing men approaching from in front of us was that the enemy was sending out an early morning patrol. My finger was on the trigger, squeezing gently and holding my breath ready to go; they came so close to paying the price. It was only because of the sharp eyesight of one of our team that a tragedy was averted. After a few shouts they located us and ran to join our section.

I was about to tear a strip off them when I could see that they were obviously too far gone, gabbling incoherently. Apparently, they'd gone out on patrol the previous night and somehow managed to get themselves in between the two opposing lines. They were miles away from where they should have been, trying to find their own regiment but were glad to have found us. They were blissfully unaware of just how close they had come to being shot and killed. It doesn't bear thinking about how we would have felt if we'd shot two of our own.

We stayed in that position for a few days then pushed on into the countryside to the north of Lentini with Mount Etna visible in the distance.

It was an incredible sight and seemed a lot closer than it actually was. Scattered in the countryside were farmhouses and outbuildings which were surrounded by dry stone walling and these huge fences made from cactus plants, which must have been twelve feet high or more. The cactus reminded me of the old comi-cut pictures that we used to see in newspapers; big oval shaped leaves covered in spikes with cactus pears. We cleared the farmhouse and took up our positions; it covered a large amount of land including the house, various outbuildings and a dry well in the farmyard. Sergeant Errington and Lance Corporal Till occupied the dry well, whilst Rennie and I positioned ourselves by the dry stone wall underneath the cactus.

We hadn't been there long when we came under attack from German mortar bombs. After the first bomb dropped, I immediately thought that we'd dropped right into range of one of the German positions, and that we should be getting out of there as soon as possible. One of the bombs in the first salvo fell either directly onto or next to the dry stone well and Sergeant Errington was killed. I don't know if Till was wounded but he jumped out of there and ran across the farmyard straight through the cactus hedge and over the dry stone wall. He then ran like hell down the hill heading towards the regimental aide post which was two miles away, but the Red Cross post was clearly visible from our position.

The last I saw of him was his blond hair disappearing down the valley as he bobbed in and out of the shrubbery.

Although we felt reasonably safe behind the stone wall, and were well dug in, something made me feel uneasy and I told Rennie that we should vacate the area. But by then the second salvo was on its way. The bombs fell in salvos of six and we decided to stick it out until after the sixth bomb. We counted the impact of each bomb hoping that none of them would land on top of us. Luckily for us that didn't happen and as soon as the sixth had dropped, we threw the gun and magazines on top of the wall, jumped over, and ran like hell for the rocks but when we were halfway there the German gunner spotted us and sprayed us with machine gun bullets. Fortunately, his bullets fell behind us as we ran and we made it safely to the rocks, which continued to be peppered with machine gun fire.

We had to lie there for over an hour waiting until the tide of battle had flowed over. We were then able to stand up and take stock of our situation and decided to return to check on the farm buildings. Where once there stood a sturdy stone wall that we had to climb over, there was now a gap enabling us to walk straight through. The wall and all the cacti had been completely demolished along with all of the farm buildings. Nothing would have been able to survive in there.

Rennie and I looked at each other knowingly; realising just how close we had come to death, and he assured me that from then on, he would trust my judgement on any future decisions. I'm sure others would have made the same decision to move out of there, but it was still very comforting to know that I'd done the right thing. Of course, had I not made that decision I wouldn't be here to relate this account.

When this battle was over, we moved from our position and started to advance with Mount Etna ahead of us. Since landing at Avola it always seemed that we were heading straight for Etna but it was just that it happened to coincide and be in the line of our advance.

Primosole Bridge

Our instructions were to reach the first wet river in Sicily, the River Simeto. In July 1943 British paratroopers were waiting to be dropped into Sicily; their objective being the Primosole Bridge. They successfully took out the Italian garrisons at the bridge. However, the Germans had already dropped an elite group of their own paratroopers because they also realised the strategic importance of the bridge. I later learnt that these were the battle-hardened 'Fallschirmjaeger' troops, sometimes known as the 'Green Devils'.

The British paras drop didn't go too well and were too scattered with only a small percentage making it to the bridge itself; they fought well but were running out of ammunition and so the decision was made to pull back.

Then the task of taking this river and the bridge that crossed it was given to the men of the Durham Light Infantry. This was one of the many regiments that made up the British Army at the time. Although each of these regiments was based in their own area, the men that served in them could come from all over the country. So in the Durhams it was possible to have men from as far afield as Kent, Scotland, Wales or Cornwall for example. But each and every one of them had a great allegiance to their respective regiment.

If we had done one operation less and reached the river first it would have been down to us to take the bridge. We had been probing the area looking for the river but in the event the task of taking it fell to the Durhams. It turned out to be one of the bloodiest battles I had the good fortune to not have been part of. That's just how the cookie crumbled.

We took up our position just south of the river and the Durhams passed through us in the early hours, and took up their positions ready to assault the river crossing at midnight. The river was about as wide as the River Wear at Chester-Le-Street which is approximately 150 feet. There were steep banks on either side covered in very tall reeds; in fact, some of them were head height and a person could be completely hidden in them.

Spanning the river was a metal bridge, the Primosole Bridge, which reminded me of the bridge at Fatfield near Washington in County Durham.

Primosole Bridge (Daily Mail)

Fatfield Bridge (Sunderland Echo)

As I said previously, the Germans had dropped one of their crack paratrooper regiments at the bridge. They had taken up position overlooking the river in the cover of the reeds. When the Durhams began their assault, they were waiting for them and one of the bloodiest battles of the war ensued. I could only imagine the bitter hand to hand fighting that went on before the Durhams finally overwhelmed the German paratroopers.

The achievements of the Durham Light Infantry that night cannot be underestimated because those paratroopers were the cream of the German army. They had been sent there to fight until the end, to try and take control of the bridge, so that the rest of their army could pull back over the Messina Straits. But that night it was the Durhams that were victorious.

It was one of the highest and most courageous achievements that had been my privilege to witness, and I wondered if we would have been able to do the job that the Durham Light Infantry did that night. We were very close by waiting in case they called on us for assistance. How they didn't call for help I'll never know as we could hear the battle going on and it seemed like every yard of ground had to be fought for by hand to hand combat, before they finally took control of the bridge.

A monument was erected at the Primosole Bridge for the men of the Durham Light Infantry and occasionally I meet people who either had a relative, or had simply heard of someone that died at Primosole. They couldn't possibly have any real comprehension of the achievement of those brave men, and the losses that they sustained.

I personally believe that every man who took part in that particular assault was deserving of the V.C. at the very least. Because we had to advance through the position after it had been taken to consolidate it, and we saw the carnage for ourselves.

We dug in among the reeds in an area which was given the name 'stinky valley' because when the sun came up and warmed up the bodies that were still lying where they fell, the stench was unbearable. We had to get a bulldozer to clear them as it was impossible to find them, as they were well hidden in the reeds. Once the bulldozer had done its job, we were then able to cover the bodies to reduce the risk of disease spreading. We would go on sorties through the reeds down to the river, and one morning about two days after the battle, Rennie and I were out on patrol when we came upon a dead German paratrooper still lying behind his gun in the reeds. He had a bayonet sticking out from his back, still with the rifle attached. I imagine that he had been stumbled upon accidently and the bayonet had been plunged in a hurry. It did seem odd that the rifle had been left behind, but it was a reminder of how bitter and ferocious the fighting was in this encounter.

No praise is too great for the lads that fought in the battle for Primosole. It was 'the battle' of Sicily to me, and it opened the way for the Army to move on to Messina. Not taking this bridge would have had an incalculable effect upon future operations. Coming from County Durham myself I couldn't help but feel an enormous sense of pride, and deemed it a privilege to have been associated with them.

We moved out and headed towards Catania, one of the largest towns in Sicily. It lies at the foot of Mount Etna with a plain in front known as the Catania Plain. This was the last battle in Sicily that our division was to take part in, and we dug ourselves in on the plain to await further developments.

Soon afterwards we received a visit from our brigadier who I would describe as a harum-scarum individual. Although we had lots of derogatory nicknames for him, such as Shaggy, Shag Nasty, or Ginger, because of his mass of ginger hair, he was actually held in high regard by the whole brigade. Mainly because of the way that he showed readiness to be in the firing line and we quite enjoyed his outspokenness. Until that day I hadn't had any close contact with him; he was there to inspect the divisions and their positions ahead of the battle for Catania.

As he approached our section, we were a little apprehensive about what he was going to say. We were dug in with our guns at the ready; he tapped one of the guns with his walking stick and said, "What would you do if the Germans came running across that field?" There was a very brief pause then in unison we said, "Kill them, sir." He replied with, "That's the idea. Don't take any prisoners--kill the bastards!" That was the kind of situation that he relished. Then, as he walked closer to me, accompanied by Claude Hull, he asked if there was anything that we wanted. As it happened, we had absolutely no cigarettes at all, and so I thought 'In for a penny in for a pound' and informed the brigadier. During the war cigarettes were considered to be a staple part of the Army's provisions, so he expressed his horror to Claude Hull and promised that we would have our cigarettes by the afternoon.

Sure enough the afternoon came and we were each issued with thirty cigarettes. I wasn't sure what Claude Hull's opinion on the matter was, but I remember thinking at the time that he could go to hell; the men were deserving of those cigarettes as they had all entered into many battles without the comforts that they were entitled to; some of them sharing 'dog ends'. The fact that as soon as the brigadier realised we had no cigarettes and they were forthcoming, proved to us that they were available if someone only had the inclination to put in a request. So we got our cigarettes and I will always remember 'Shag' for that.

As I said, we were dug in on the Catania Plain and as we lay there, the smoke from Mount Etna was clearly visible. We had to probe the area in front of us as we advanced towards Etna, checking for the enemy. Whilst out on patrol one day we were crossing through some orange groves and had only just entered the groves when suddenly an Italian soldier jumped out waving a white flag. He was fortunate that we didn't immediately shoot him. He wanted us to follow him, and was gesturing in the direction that he wanted us to go. Obviously, we were very cautious and prodded him to lead the way. He then led us to a glade deep in the centre of the orange grove. Here we found two trestle tables covered with white tablecloths on top of which were bottles of wine and dishes of nuts. There were about fifteen Italians and it turned out they were waiting to surrender; the wine was there open and ready, waiting for the first British troops to get there.

We were still unsure of the situation, keeping one eye open watching for any treachery, but there was nothing to worry about. They just wanted to give themselves up as they could see that the British were taking control of Sicily. One of them even wanted to join us to fight the Germans who were once his ally; this of course was out of the question and as he was sticking with us, we had to eventually forcibly eject him.

The political situation at the time was the Italians had given up and wanted the whole thing to be over with, now that their allies the Germans were not doing so well. Previously they had wanted to be aligned with the successful German expeditions. I couldn't help but temper their current behaviour with what had passed before. Although I wouldn't describe the Italians as a warlike race, I found it difficult to understand their political stance, which led them to take up arms on Germany's side in the first place. But that's all water under the bridge now.

We went on probing the area, and fought a couple more skirmishes and then after a few 'house to house' sorties, Catania fell to us. After its capitulation we were given permission to have a look around part of the town; only part because three quarters of it was out of bounds to troops. There was really nothing to see; the shops were in no position to do any trading, and so all in all the visit to Catania was a bit of a damp fizz.

111

Letojanni

We moved forward along the coast road passing various villages on the way and eventually came to a small fishing village called Letojanni, which was situated approximately 25 miles south of Messina. It was decided that the B.H.Q. would be billeted in one of the empty houses and we were given a large abandoned building that had either been a hotel or civic centre. Firstly, we had to clean it up as it was in an absolute mess.

Hostilities had ceased but one of our brigades had pushed on ahead over the Messina straits to take up and form a beachhead on the other side. This was to provide protection for the rest of the army and supplies as they passed through, just as a precaution against any counterattack. Apart from that the campaign was virtually over and we were to take up our positions in the billet which we had cleaned out.

Our billet was right on the entrance road to the village of Letojanni and the entire transport heading to Italy, including both British and American had to pass us by. Also General Montgomery, whom we had met previously during the desert campaign, frequented the road quite often and so we had to post guards outside of the B.H.Q.

In the middle of Letojanni was the village square which acted as the focal point for any village activity and it was surrounded by palm trees; they were quite spectacular with 'vinegar bottle' shaped trunks. We used the square to mount the guard where we performed an exhibition ceremony for the incoming and outgoing guards. The whole village turned out to watch the guard being changed, and we took great pride on making sure we were well turned out, and the guard was well presented. We wanted to put on a good show and they certainly seemed to enjoy it.

There were whitewashed gate pillars at the entrance to the village and as was common in the Army, these were smothered with battle honours. At night on guard duty we would often sit and lean against these pillars to rest our weary backs.

The B.H.Q. was in frequent use by the officers where they would maybe discuss plans, but also the officers' mess was in there. They would wander towards us in the dark whereupon we would shout out, "Halt, who goes there?" Although we knew who it was, we took great delight in scaring them. They also knew who we were, and that we wouldn't hesitate to put a bullet in them. A lot of mischievous pleasure was derived from hearing how quickly they shouted out their names! That still brings back a smile to my face thinking about it, even after all of these years. Of course it also provided us with a bit of light relief during the long nights on guard duty.

As I said earlier, in the early hours during the night on guard duty we would often rest up against the pillars, but what we were not aware of was that our backs were getting covered in the whitewashed battle honours. In the morning after mounting the guard, we were accused of lounging around, which of course we denied, but the evidence was plainly there for all to see!

When we were not on guard duty we did lounge around, because there was not much else to do apart from watch the army transport passing along the road. As this was the only road it got very busy at times. On one of these occasions whilst we were sitting chatting, the regimental sergeant major turned up. With a great sense of urgency he informed us that we would be called to attention in about an hour's time. He was pleading with us to do our best and not let him down, but we had no idea what the panic was about. An hour passed and we duly presented ourselves when who should arrive in his staff car but Montgomery. He got out of his car and we presented arms whilst he did an inspection.

I was struck by his bright blue eyes that seemed to have a twinkle in them. He looked to me to be someone with a sense of humour, although I couldn't be certain that this was the case. He inspected the guard and said all the non-committal things that these fellows always said; asking if we were alright, "Good show" and all that balls. He inspected the guard and everything was immaculate; I don't know if it was the occasion, but for once it all ran smoothly and no one put a foot wrong.

After the visit was over the R.S.M. was full of praise; he was absolutely overjoyed to the extent that he was even putting his arms around us, and as a reward we were given a right good feed.

The only other occasion that I had any contact with our Commander in Chief was one day when we happened to be lounging around chatting outside of our billet. There were three of us just sitting talking, kicking the sand about with our feet, when one of the lads spotted a car coming over the little bridge that was opposite our billet. He realised straight away that it was Montgomery, who then pulled up and called us over. We immediately thought we were going to get a dressing down for lounging about. As it happened we were worrying needlessly because when we got to the car, he simply asked us how we were fixed for cigarettes.

When he heard that we didn't have any he said, "Well it just so happens that I have a girlfriend in England and she sends me quite a lot, so I'm sure I can spare a few." With that he rummaged in the back of his vehicle and produced some packets; he passed over about 150 in total and said, "No doubt I'll see you again", and drove off.

On our return to the billet, we told the rest of the men that Montgomery had given us some cigarettes, but they didn't believe us and just laughed. However, they eventually realised that Montgomery was probably the only person they could have come from. From then on, the men would take turns to sit outside, hoping that lightning would strike twice, but it never did.

We spent our time wandering round the village and visiting the beach, but we had to choose our spot carefully as the sanitation in the area wasn't brilliant. We discovered that the villagers used the beach as their toilet, and it was left to the incoming tide to clean it up. The beach itself was not that good, consisting mainly of pebbles and was quite rocky, but the sea itself was gloriously warm and the water clear, which made swimming very enjoyable.

Fish were in abundance and we did our fishing with hand grenades, although of course this was very much frowned upon. Some of the villagers would open their doors to sell us wine and a few nuts in their attempt to make a little money; we were glad of this even though it was just a coarse vino.

Apart from that there was very little fraternisation with the locals, especially the young women of the village. Some of our more romantically inclined men did try to befriend the girls, but their menfolk were extremely protective towards them. They strongly discouraged the girls from any socializing with us and tried as much as possible to keep them out of sight.

Personally, I wasn't particularly bothered and along with a few others, would occupy my time exploring the countryside, climbing up into the hills among the peaches, oranges and pears. Occasionally we would happen upon some small cottages inhabited by very poor peasants who seemed to exist solely on the drying of figs; these were on trays outside drying in the sun. They were very poor and although we didn't have much ourselves, if we had the odd sweet, bar of chocolate or cigarette to give them they were really grateful.

It had been made clear to us that we were not advancing into Italy but for the moment were to stay in Sicily. Our days had become very relaxed and there was almost a holiday atmosphere. There was even talk of the possibility of it becoming a holiday camp as respite for the soldiers that had been fighting in Italy with us staying behind to organise things. Obviously this idea went down very well with us, and we even began to stop thinking about the war, what had passed and what the future held; the idea of being stuck in a holiday camp suited us very nicely!

However, all good things must come to an end and sometimes sooner than expected; it wasn't long before the whole division was called to a conference in the middle of the surrounding olive groves.

We were addressed by General Montgomery who said that, with the war still going on along the Italian mainland, no doubt we would be wondering what our role was to be. He informed us that we had not been forgotten about and that it had been decided that, along with the 7th Armoured Division and the 51st Highland Division, we were to return to England in the very near future, to begin training for the forthcoming invasion of Europe.

Our division, the 50th, had been chosen as the assault division for the invasion and he told us that he knew we wouldn't let him down in the forthcoming campaign and hoped to see us very soon back in Blighty.

That was basically the end of the Sicilian campaign and it was time to sort out and collect our gear together. We would have liked to have some sort of keepsake to remember the place, but as I have already explained it was a very poor area with very little to buy. I picked a couple of lemons and found a few almonds which I stuffed in my kit bag as keepsakes to take back to England. Then we headed about 50 miles north to Augusta, to embark and return to England and begin training for the invasion of Europe.

When I look back on the Sicilian campaign, I remember it for the beauty of the island, the warm sea, the climate, and the balmy moonlit nights. On some evenings we used to sit on the flat roof of our billet accompanied by a couple of the

Sicilian villagers, who used to play some favourite Italian tunes on their violins and accordions.

The nights were warm, sultry warm, and the air was filled with the smell of the surrounding countryside and the abundance of fruit trees, grapevines and olive trees. We could almost have forgotten that we had been fighting a war.

The campaign itself hadn't been too bad for me, but apart from the beauty of the place, the thing that sticks in my mind is the Battle of Primosole and the brave men of the Durham Light Infantry. Many of whom lost their lives. This conflicted with my overall memory of Sicily, which seemed a place more suited as a holiday destination than for a war. I have often thought that I would like to return someday, but I suppose some of the areas that we had full access to, like Taormina, will have reverted back to being the holiday destinations of the wealthy like they once were.

So that for me was the end of the Sicilian campaign and it was time to move on to prepare for the next.

Training for D-Day

It was with some trepidation that we returned back to England to begin our training for the forthcoming invasion of Europe. The next part of my story covers the events prior to my being wounded during that campaign.

We arrived in England at Liverpool on November 4th 1943 at 3am; we disembarked into a warehouse on the dockside and then boarded a train which took us to a forest in Norfolk. It wasn't the welcome that we had expected after serving abroad in the desert and Sicily. We had been led to believe that we were heroes and expected to be greeted as such, but it was somewhat of an anti-climax as no one in England knew of our return.

We settled down to the routine of life in barracks during wartime; it was at this time that I received my promotion to full corporal for services apparently not rendered. I had got into some trouble and been rebuked by the RSM for constantly leaving camp in the company of my bosom pal Rennie. After receiving the reprimand from the RSM I requested that I be demoted so both Rennie and I had to go before the Commanding Officer. It didn't turn out at all as I had expected as he promoted me to full Corporal, and Rennie was given a Lance Corporal stripe; the judgement of Solomon indeed!

It was decided that we would be shipped north to Scotland for the necessary training; the area chosen was Inveraray on the shores of Loch Fyne.

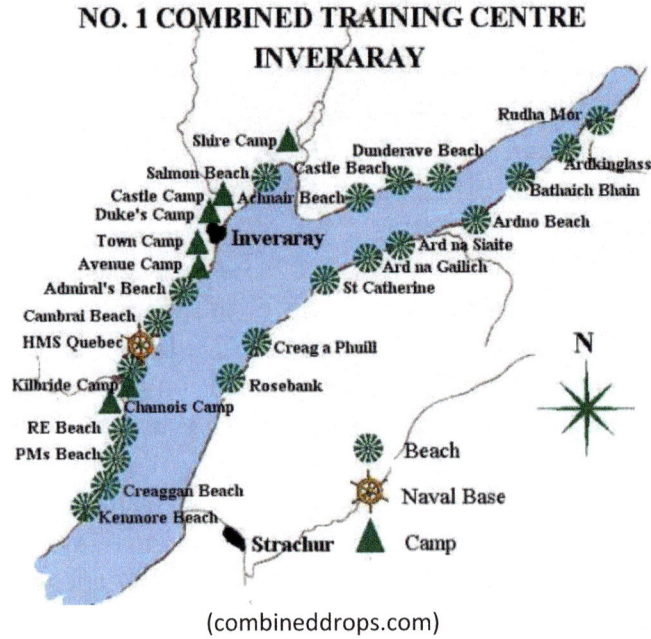

(combineddrops.com)

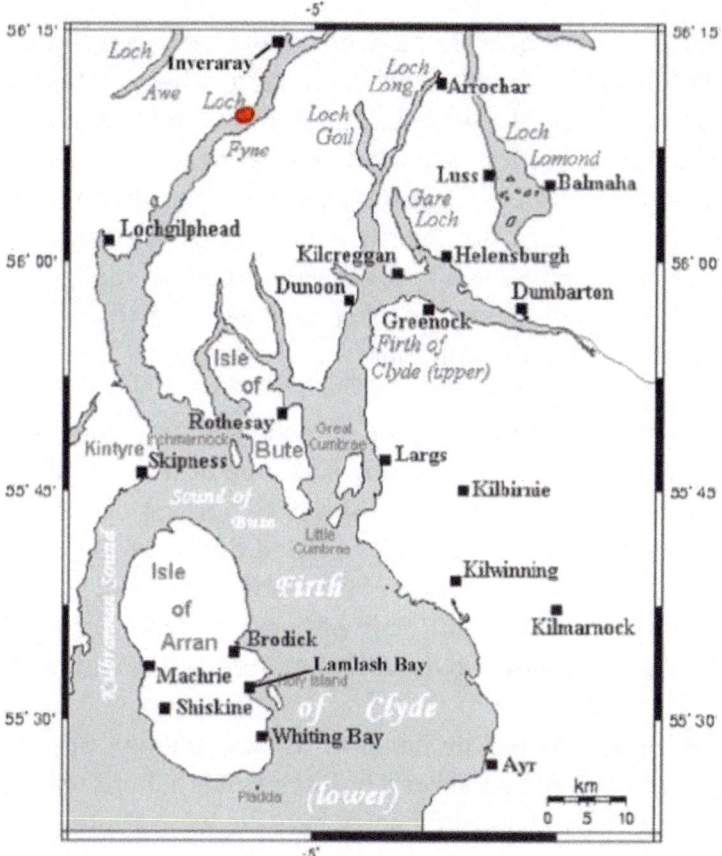

source [http://www.aquarius.geomar.de/omc/make map.html here]

122

All combined operations were there and after our first briefing we were left in no doubt as to what our task on D-Day was to be; we were told that we were to be an assault battalion and after leaving the briefing we all felt pretty down in the mouth. Naturally we had expected to take part in the invasion, but because of all our previous service abroad, I suppose we thought we'd be more molly coddled and we certainly didn't expect to have to be the first to set foot on the beaches on that fateful morning.

Nevertheless we were used to such setbacks and we soon buckled down to our training; the type of training that we'd never before experienced. The first morning of training we went down to the loch and boarded boats the like of which we had not seen before and we made our way over the very choppy and very cold loch; we were halfway across when the R.A.F. screamed over us and obliterated us with smoke.

This was followed by small arms fire opening up and we thought D-Day had arrived before we were quite ready. We landed on the opposite bank where we were strafed, shelled and machine gunned; we began to wonder that if this was just the training what the hell the real thing was going to be like.

We lost two men during that training and felt very bitter about it. We stayed with combined ops for a few weeks and before we left we had another briefing.

123

At this briefing we were told what our task would be; I personally thought it a bit risky to entrust so many people with the kind of information that we'd been given.

Combined Operations Camp
(wavynavy.blogspot.com)

Landing Craft training

Photo - Capt. W.T. Lockeyear, IWM.

We Return to the South Coast

We travelled to the south of England to continue our training knowing without any doubt what would be expected of us in the coming months.

We resumed our training on the landing craft and invaded just about every town on the south coast! Hayling Island, Weymouth Bay to name but two; it seemed like we were in and out of Weymouth Bay a thousand times creeping around the beaches in the early hours. We came and went like ghosts in the night. We lived with the landing craft and were seasick, frozen, soaked, and absolutely drenched day after day. The weather was foul and we were living chock-a-block together.

As yet we had not been given the date of the actual invasion but everything seemed to be coming to a climax during the early summer. One could feel that something was about to happen. Things were really building up in the south; every road was blocked with trucks, guns, and tanks. Everywhere one went you would find troops on the move.

Every day we were away on the landing craft returning at night in full view of the townspeople, but they were so used to our comings and goings that they scarcely raised an eyebrow.

126

This preparation was all part and parcel of the grand strategy although we still didn't really know what was going on, but felt that very soon something was going to happen. Sure enough one morning instead of going on our usual manoeuvres we were confined to camp.

It was a large camp and as often was the case in such camps, there were quite a lot of civilians employed in various positions. They were allowed in on that particular morning but then that was it. No one regardless of rank or status was permitted to go outside the perimeter. The arguments were strong and fierce but the shutters were down and they were to stay like that until we were on the other side of the channel.

Briefing began almost immediately and I was detailed to load our three 15 cwt trucks along with a list of requirements down to the last bullet; I had to do this without the help of the storeman who had left some time ago. I had visions of staying with these trucks but my hopes were dashed by the C.O. who informed us that our section was to remain after the trucks were loaded. The briefing was very thorough and we studied aerial photographs of our objective. The R.A.F had done an excellent job getting the photos because they were extremely sharp and detailed and would help us to take our objective.

We were tasked on D-Day with landing and making our way to a copse on some high ground about seven miles inland; once there we were to take prisoners that were wanted urgently by intelligence back in England. The troops guarding the area were known as smoke troops firing smoke mortars to aid concealment, but our company had to push through it and get there regardless even if we only managed to get one prisoner. Knowing my companions from previous sorties I thought we'd have trouble hanging onto one! As I look back now to those events it is difficult to visualise just how ruthless we had become.

Returning to the briefings I was a little cynical about certain aspects of the enterprise. Some of our officers were inexperienced in battle and we had new junior officers. Our commanding officer had never seen a shot fired in anger, yet looked on the whole affair with extreme optimism and impatience to get on with things. He laughed at my pessimism and caution; he was such a gentleman that I was reluctant to dampen his enthusiasm.

I had no illusions about our friends with the jackboots; they were professionals, I'd met them in the dessert and in Sicily and I knew that every inch of ground would have to be fought over.

Throughout all of the briefings I tried to prepare the ignorant as to what to expect; expect the worst then reality wouldn't be so bad.

Whilst all this was going on my pal Rennie was in Winchester hospital with malaria which he'd contracted on leaving Sicily, and I expected to be joining him. But try as I might I was unable to raise a sweat or get my temperature up one jot! I did think as we'd spent all our time together day and night then I would catch it too; but it wasn't to be and Rennie stayed on in Winchester whilst I continued with the unit to Europe. Before we were confined to barracks I was able to visit Rennie in the hospital and impressed on him the need for him to stay in hospital as long as possible; I was apprehensive about what could happen during the initial landings and I had enough to worry about looking after myself, without having to be worrying about Rennie. We were very close; closer than I'd ever been to any person.

At this time we had with us two Norwegian lads. Although their English was limited they had trained with us on the assault crafts and the various training exploits up until the time of the invasion proper. Unfortunately they were not allowed, for some inexplicable reason, to land with us on D-Day but were to land two or three days later; why this was I never could understand.

One reason why I am mentioning these two Norwegians is because I believe there are a great many people who have the impression that it was only the British and Americans fighting this war for the conquest of Europe. However there were so many other nationalities taking part, voluntarily doing their bit to help liberate the countries that had been over-run.

I only ever met those two Norwegians but I held them in the highest regard. They certainly were a credit to their nation. The reason we had the Norwegians with us in our unit was because King Haakon of Norway was the Colonel in Chief of our regiment, the Green Howards, sometimes referred to as the Princess of Wales' own Yorkshire Regiment.

Troops from the 6th or 7th Battalion, Green Howards
embarking onto the Empire Lance

After a couple more days in the camp we were to spend one afternoon tidying up and burning any rubbish that we had accumulated. Then in the evening after dark, we boarded our transport and headed for the dockside; there we were to board the mother ship for the final time. The mother ship was one of four that were allocated to our particular beach; we were to land in Normandy on Gold Beach which was the code name for one of the five areas of the Allied invasion in German occupied France. Gold Beach was positioned in the middle of the five designated areas.

The mother ships all had the prefix Empire and the one I was on was called Empire Lance. On boarding we went below decks and found ourselves in a metal welded construction with bunks on a sort of rack folded against the sides, which permitted easy access. Naturally down came the bunks, off came our gear and we sprawled about on our bunks smoking, chatting and discussing what lay ahead for us.

My section, although normally comprising of seven men, had an extra man for this operation; we had an extra light machine gun carried by a commando. There always seemed to be a certain amount of glamour surrounding commandos and they did a pretty useful job so we were expecting something special. They were very proficient in the use of these weapons, but apart from that I personally didn't think they seemed to be any different to anyone else, and subsequent events did not cause me to alter my opinion.

I also had two very young eighteen year olds and they had as yet to see any active service; they were full of questions regarding what to expect, something that I found really difficult to deal with. It wasn't possible to truly convey what actual combat means; the over-riding emotion was one of fear which you could almost taste, and there was a physical pain with it like indigestion. Telling young lads this wouldn't have exactly inspired them.

We spent the rest of the evening playing cards, chatting, and obviously worrying about what the morning would bring. As it happened we needn't have worried, because when morning arrived the weather was pretty rough, and word came round that the operation, which was initially scheduled for the 5th June, had been cancelled.
We were all a little relieved if I'm honest, and we thought perhaps we would be returning to port, leaving the invasion for another day. It was a bit of an anti-climax, but I was never one to look a gift horse in the mouth!

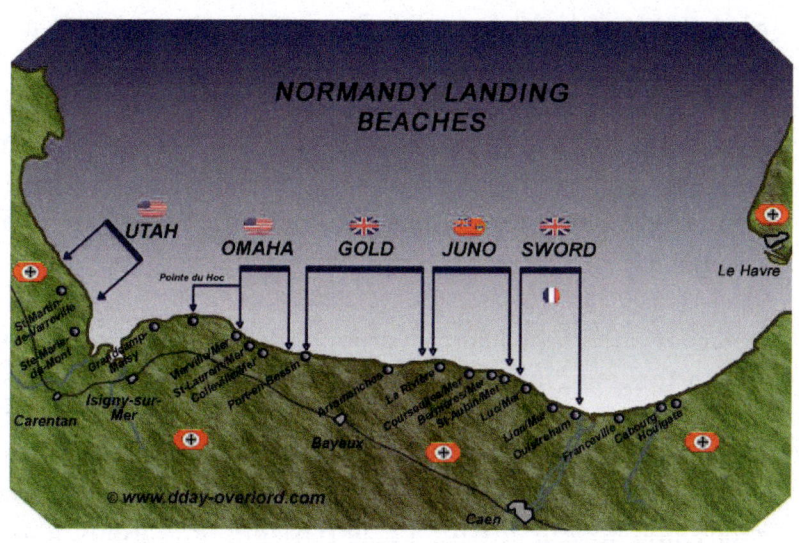

The Beaches of D-Day

The Landing

Daylight came the next day and although I personally couldn't see much of an improvement in the weather, we were given the information that the operation was to go ahead. So, on the morning of the 6th June 1944, we received our orders and off we went into the channel; everything was planned down to the last detail and hopefully to perfection. All timetables had to be exactly the same and watches synchronised. Our landing time on Gold Beach was to be 7.25 that morning. There wasn't much to see, just a conglomeration of boats and I found that I was reflecting more on my immediate surroundings than what lay ahead.

However, I did feel a certain amount of apprehension about the forthcoming assault; I felt that I'd done my time. This was to be the third campaign that I was partaking in; I was regarded as a veteran, and in a unit such as mine veterans didn't last forever. We had been reinforced innumerable times due to our losses; I'd left friends in various burial grounds mainly in the desert, and many were wounded too severely to return.

I felt it was only a matter of time before my number came up. We all tried to convince ourselves that it wouldn't happen to us, but if we weighed up the percentages then our time was limited; we could only hope that we were wounded slightly, preferably in the rear end, something not life threatening. Of course that was not our choice to make and I personally would be approaching that beach with a certain amount of fear.

When we reached the anchorage point for the large craft the weather had abated somewhat but the sea had a heavy swell and the boat was swaying from side to side; it was still early morning and the sun was just trying to break through.

We came up on deck in single file and boarded the assault craft with all of our gear as one would a lifeboat, and it was then lowered over the side into the water on davits. That in itself was quite perilous. There were two seamen on each side controlling the davits, and it was their job when the boat swung out, to drop it down and stop it from crashing against the side.

Unfortunately when we were only halfway down there was a huge swell and we were thrown about; we banged into the side with such force that I thought we were going to end up overboard, so I began to loosen my belt in preparation for my dive into the sea. I was a reasonable swimmer but would have sunk straight to the bottom if I was carrying the gear, so I was prepared to dump the lot and swim for it. Suddenly the boat swung the other way, and then it dropped about 6 feet down into the water. It was a terrible sensation being a flat bottomed boat, it felt something like a lift with its cables broken dropping rapidly, we hit the water with a resounding SMACK!

Then we had to contend with the supporting block and tackle that was uncoupled by the two seamen and which proceeded to fly through the air into the middle of us; we had to be pretty nippy to avoid it.

We checked the boat over and everything seemed okay and so the engine was started and we pulled away from the side of the mother craft; we waited a few minutes until all the other assault craft had been jettisoned then we all moved off together towards our rendezvous.

By this time the sky was absolutely thick with aircraft. The light aircraft were flying in and out on sorties and high in the sky we could see the Flying Fortresses. They were probably bombing the rear of the beachhead to prevent any reinforcements getting through after we had made our landing.

The airborne had already gone in the night before and it was our intention, after taking Bayeux, to link up with them. However the timetables were slightly off and so we were unsuccessful in that regard.

I was somewhat surprised at how long our journey to the beach was taking because I was only expecting it to last a few minutes. But it was quite a long haul and a few people were being seasick. We were all issued with seasick pills, which I took as a matter of course, but some of the lads hadn't taken theirs. I don't think I was actually capable of being sick, as I had such a knot in my stomach due to the apprehension building up about what lay ahead.

If there was anyone on that boat with absolutely no illusions of what to expect then that person would have been me. Having been through many battles before, I was confident of being able to give a good account of myself. However, no one could say for certain in advance how you would actually perform, because in a battle situation everything was done instinctively, with no time to plan ahead. This is what occupied my mind on the journey across to France.

Initially it was pretty quiet; no one was firing at us, and I was looking around to see what was visible on the sea and in the sky. We could see our aircraft going in, and to our left there was Juno beach which was the responsibility of the Canadians. To the left of Juno was Sword, and this was to be taken by the British. Rocket firing barges were going in towards Sword Beach and they were setting off a terrific number of rockets. I believe they carried about 350 on each barge and it seemed like they had all gone off together. The air was full of rockets and with the weight of destruction that was piling down on those beaches it was hard to imagine that anything would be left standing.

However we had been in this sort of a position before and no matter how much we rained down armaments on the Germans, it seemed like there were always more to fight. I was wishing that some of those rockets were directed to our beach; I certainly would have been a lot happier if some of that activity was directed to our front.

I wasn't permitted to stay there stargazing the whole time and had to get back below. There was a sort of half-deck that allowed the people in charge of the craft to move about over our heads, and it was important that we didn't get in their way.

As we were approaching the beach I could already see a landing craft grounded; it just reached the beach when the whole lot exploded. It was awful to see; flames and smoke were shooting about 150 foot in the air. This was the first craft to touch land and whether it had hit a mine or received a direct hit I wasn't too sure, but I thought the explosion looked like it might have been a direct hit from an 88 millimetre.

The sea was very choppy as we were nearing the beaches and preparing for 'ramps down'. I'd been expecting to feel the bottom of the boat grinding on dry land but that didn't happen. The command was given ramps down, but there was no dry land and the first section ran out in single file. As each man got to the end of the ramp there seemed to be some hesitation and it was only when it was my turn that I could see why this was. I was leading the second section and when I got onto the ramp the last man from the first section was still standing at the end of the ramp; I was right behind him but he didn't move so I said "Come on John" and gave him a gentle push. He had obviously been hit with shrapnel or something as he stood there, and fell into the water surrounded by blood.

I stepped off the boat and thought I was going to meet Father Neptune as the water came right up to my shoulders, and covered all the gear that I was carrying. In fact there was only my head and a little bit of shoulder protruding and so I turned to the sailor on the craft and said "Could you not get the bloody boat a bit closer?" He did look somewhat astounded but it seemed a bit ridiculous to me that we were so far out from the shore and the water was that deep. There was a lot of debris floating in the water and also stakes dug into the bottom with only about a foot visible.

I started to move forward as best I could with shells hitting the water straight ahead of me. When the shells hit, shrapnel flew off and skimmed across the sea towards me. It reminded me of someone skimming pebbles at the beach but these were far more dangerous, and with only my head and shoulders above the waterline it was quite disconcerting seeing them bouncing towards me.

As I was moving forward I came upon a commando who shouted "I'm wounded, I'm wounded"; sure enough he had a large gash in the top of his thigh but he was still walking and the wound was not life threatening. On reflection my reaction must have seemed rather absurd as my main concern was what he had done with the L.M.G. (Light Machine Gun); he told me that he had dropped it and I just said "Oh man, what did you do that for?"

I am still amused to this day at my attitude; I know that he was wounded but that L.M.G. was a very important piece of equipment. I told him to get back on the boat, even though the assault craft were not supposed to pick people up. Their job was to get everyone off then leave, however as the last section was leaving the boat the wounded from the first were trying to get back in.

It wasn't long before my section was being hammered and one of the 18 year old lads was hit. He was carrying a Bangalore torpedo which resembled a sawn off scaffold pole and contained high explosives. These were used to slip under the barbed wire defences to blast our way through. He was heading to get back on the boat but was panicking because he still had the Bangalore torpedo. "What shall I do with this Corp?" he said, and I replied "Drop it in the water." He was too nervous to do that and so I took it from him and dropped it in the sea myself.

Bangalore Torpedoes
(paratrooper.be)

Bangalore Torpedoes in use
(d-day-overlord.com)

I was still groping around in the water trying to find the L.M.G. dropped by the commando and eventually I was fortunate enough to find it. To say that I was relieved is something of an understatement as we were all carrying the magazines for this gun and without it we would have been 'up the creek'. I emptied out the water from the gun and proceeded, amidst heavy fire, towards the beach and made it on to dry land. I stopped beside a stake in the sand and thought that I would lean against it to get my breath back. I was leaning on the stake and on looking around I could see 2 massive mortar bombs strapped to the top! Needless to say I got out of there pretty sharpish; I was thinking if they go off now I'll be blown all the way back to England.

We started with eight in the unit; the commando was shot along with the 18 year old lad, and I knew of one more that didn't make it so I was expecting to have five left in the team. There was a knocked out tank by the water's edge so the remainder of us got behind it; it turned out that there was only three of us left and I had no idea what happened to the others.

Among the three of us there was a young lad called Ibbitson who'd also been through the desert and was a veteran like myself. We looked at each other wondering what to do next, knowing that we couldn't stay there. He pointed me to the low water mark where our C.O. was lying wounded with the company sergeant major kneeling beside him.

I said to Ibbitson that I thought the C.O. looked pretty bad, and we subsequently found out that he had been killed. There were bodies lying everywhere and I turned to Ibbitson saying "Where's the gap?"

We were supposed to have been dropped in front of a gap that the sappers had cleared ahead of us, but we were about 150 yards away from it. On assessment it looked like the personnel that hadn't made it were trying to find the gap, and had come under fire from all the artillery that was ranged down onto the beach. We decided that our only option was to go through under the barrage. Ibbitson and I were both fully aware that if we stayed where we were we had no chance.

It wasn't an easy decision to make, especially as we could see the bodies of those that had gone before us who had either been shot or caught out on mines. So we stood up and ran like hell for the dunes, which I guessed were about 150 yards away; I don't know about Ibbitson but I didn't leave any footprints in the sand on my way to those dunes!

I arrived first and dropped down behind the first dune I came to, closely followed by Ibbitson who did the same. There was no sign of the other lad, and neither of us knew what had happened to him.

Close by was another corporal who seemed completely shell-shocked; he asked if we had seen Peter Bull and we told him that we had. Peter was lying dead close to the water's edge and this really unnerved the young corporal to the point where he was no good at all.

We rested by the dunes for a while and I remembered that I had a packet of cigarettes and matches under my tin helmet of all places; I had done that for easy access but it was quite fortunate as if they had been anywhere else they would have been soaked.

Although it now seems to be a ridiculous thing to do at that time, we decided that as we had got that far, it would be a good idea to have a smoke. While we were puffing away we were planning our next move, but for the moment we weren't being fired on, as all the mortar, shells and machine gun fire was going right over our heads. So for the next couple of minutes we felt quite safe in that position, which for an infantryman was quite something.

Then along came our second in command Mr Chambers; he had been slightly wounded in the forehead and was quite shaken with blood pouring down his face. He was gathering up the rest of the company and trying to get them organised into some sort of formation and so we joined in with them.

As we were making our way through the dunes we came upon a concrete shelter, in which there were eight Royal Navy divers. They had stripped off their gear and it looked like they were wearing long johns, but in fact they were 'all in one' swimsuits. Seeing them reminded me of the fact that every part of the armed forces was involved in this war, and the divers would have arrived ahead of us trying to make safe as many of the defences as they could. They were now waiting until the first wave landed and got through before a launch would arrive to retrieve them. I waved and my gesture was returned, but I couldn't help thinking that it was small thanks for the enormous contribution they'd made that day.

We continued through the dunes with the firing of mortars and shells on both sides of us; we didn't engage as our objective was to push through into the countryside to the map reference that had been assigned to us. Then it would be time for us to do our bit. Each company had their own tasks to fulfil; some were taking out various pill boxes and strongpoints along the way and it was this that earned a good friend of mine, Sergeant Major Hollis, the V.C. for bravery.

We passed through a village into open undulating countryside which was mainly pastureland and some cornfields. We tried to keep to the hedgerows avoiding the high ground as much as possible; every so often we were fired on, but our orders were to take evasive action at that stage.

We stumbled upon a group of soldiers in German uniforms who turned out to be Polish; they came towards us with their hands up surrendering, but when they got closer we could see that a couple of them were holding hand grenades. They were very apologetic about that as we disarmed them; the war was not of their making and they didn't want to be there, but had been brought to the front as a work battalion. Still it was disconcerting nonetheless as we knew the hand grenades were not meant for the Germans. We were not interested in taking them prisoners so we sent them packing back down the line towards the beaches.

I noticed after we had passed the dunes that there were a lot of earthworks, where there had been a great deal of digging going on; there were dugouts, slit-trenches, gun emplacements you name it they'd dug it!

It made me think that if the timing of the invasion had been later and the German army had more time to prepare, we would have paid an even heavier price on those beaches. The earthworks would have been occupied by soldiers and the defences would therefore have been much stronger because the extent of the earthworks that were in progress was nobody's business.

147

This was one of the thoughts that occurred to me as we were advancing towards our objective.

Whilst making our way forward we were fired on four or five times; it was mainly snipers who obviously thought they had a good vantage point and were taking pot shots at us. We went forward and must have covered about two and a half miles and were to consolidate on some high ground. Most of the lads were on one side of the high ground and I got half way across when a machine gun opened up and splattered the side of the hill.

I would normally have been off like a rabbit but on this occasion I was caught on the wrong foot and completely froze; I didn't feel scared but I was unable to move one limb. The machine gun fire was whizzing loudly around my head and the lads were shouting at me to move, but for what seemed like ages, maybe about twenty seconds, I froze, and was simply unable to move. They couldn't understand it because I was laughing at the time. In instances such as that, time seems to stand still, but in reality it was probably only a matter of a few seconds before I suddenly found my limbs again and was off to join the rest of the lads; later we all had a good laugh about that.

It happened to everyone sooner or later if you were caught on the wrong foot. This was a completely foreign experience for me and most surprising, after all I'd already been through. As I said I didn't feel frightened, I'd already been through far too much to be scared.

It showed me that we are only human and subject to human frailties; it was a good thing to have happened in a way as it sharpened my mind. Although the beaches were now well behind us I am of the opinion that my behaviour that day was a delayed reaction to what had gone on earlier.

I'd seen it happen to other people, but this was the first and thankfully the last time it happened to me; I thought perhaps this sort of reaction should be investigated in more detail by those in the medical profession. In fact I always thought that there should be a limit as to how many battles any one person should be expected to take part in. The R.A.F. had a specified number of operations their crew took part in before they were withdrawn from active service. I had previously served in both the desert and Sicily and here I was taking part in a third campaign.

There were other lads with me that had also been in the desert since the start of the war. I think it was asking too much of any man to go to the well as often as these lads were asked to do. They were drawing from a limited resource of strength and courage to the point of exhausting it.

I may have become a little cynical but I don't think the powers that be were as concerned for the crew as for the aircraft; whereas with us we didn't have any valuable equipment to worry about, we just had manpower and that was expendable. This is just my own personal opinion but so many of these lads performed above and beyond what should ever have been expected of them.

Let's get back to the job in hand. We got over the high ground and consolidated our company. At that point we were also joined by two Sherman tanks, D.D.'s as they were called.

They were able to float because of an ingenious design involving a canvas skirt and propellers, and their real name was Sherman Duplex Drive. However both the British and American military subsequently gave them the nickname Donald Ducks.

Sherman D.D.

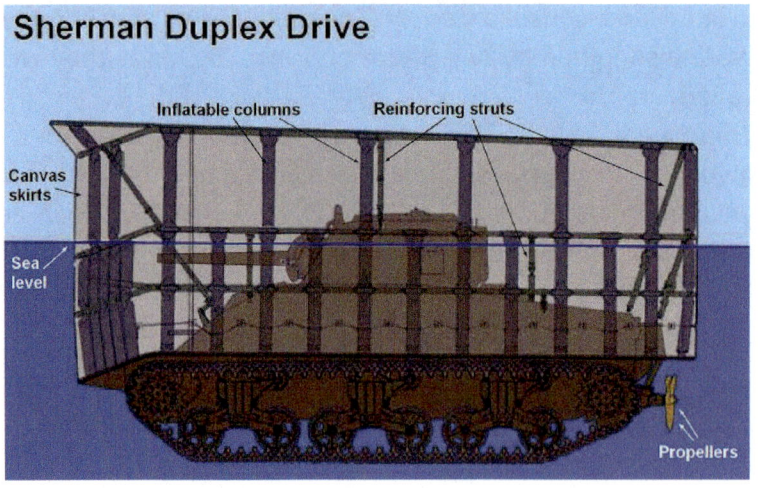

The tanks were to accompany us to our objective and this gave us quite a lift. We hadn't really worked alongside heavy armour before and loved having them at our disposal. We couldn't wait to put them to work. As we rolled along the countryside we were constantly scanning for possible threats which the tanks could take out for us with their huge guns. Their noise made it impossible for us to attract the attention of the gunner and so therefore we were supplied with coloured 2 inch mortars to be fired in the direction of the target, which was quickly followed by a shell from the tank. We were filled with a certain amount of confidence in our ability to take out our targets with the help of those two tanks.

On the aerial photographs that we'd studied prior to the landings we had seen that there was an area of discoloured ground in a pasture field that we had to cross. We believed that this was a tunnel leading to and from the spinney that we were tasked to take. Sure enough as we got about half way across the pasture, the discoloured ground was clearly visible, winding like a ribbon straight to the spinney. We whipped the guns around and slung in a couple of two inch mortar bombs straight into the spinney, then BANG, BANG, and off we went into the attack.

The tanks rumbled along so far then stopped to let us do our thing, but also remaining at the ready to direct fire on to the spinney if required. We headed for the copse with only the occasional shot coming our way; there was no machine gun fire and only one lad dropped after he'd been shot in the ankle. We kept going and made it into the copse and once there we spread out and were running around everywhere.

I saw about six German soldiers head down to what looked at first like an anti-tank ditch, but was in fact an entrance to a tunnel. They dashed into the tunnel and so I positioned myself at the bridge of the opening, loaded the Bren gun, pointed it into the tunnel and fired.

Our second Lieutenant arrived and wanted to know what was going on. When I told him what had happened he suggested that I go in after them! I told him in no uncertain language that I didn't think that was a very good idea, following it up with, "I'm not going in there, give them a few minutes and let them come out," I said.

We could hear shouting coming from inside the tunnel and then after a minute or two out walked the biggest German that I had ever seen in my life! He seemed to be about 7 feet tall and was built like a battleship; what a man! He looked to be a true Prussian complete with scar on his cheek; I'd always found Germans looked terrifying at the best of times, and this huge man appeared with his jacket slung over his shoulder in typical Teutonic fashion.

He was wearing a soft cap and riding breeches, and looked very arrogant when he strode out. However all credit to him because he was the first out and was taking quite a chance, as I'd already sent one magazine down the tunnel, and there was another one on the gun at the ready.

Out he came still wearing his revolver, with the remnants of his section following behind. We were absolutely over the moon to have captured a prisoner of his calibre; this was exactly what we were there for.

We moved to take his revolver but he had other ideas; as an officer he thought he was untouchable and felt that he should be able to keep his gun. "Get it off him" I said, "We can't have any Germans wandering around here carrying revolvers". He relinquished the revolver to the 2nd Lieutenant, which I suppose would have been a good souvenir for him, as long as he managed to take it home.

Last to come out from the tunnel were the walking wounded and they were in a sorry plight; I saw at first-hand the results of my own workmanship and was immediately filled with remorse. It was a rare occasion that anyone was confronted with the results of their own actions as I was on that day. I knew that I was responsible for all of the wounds that had been inflicted upon them, and wanted to do as much for those lads as I could. Although realistically there wasn't much I could do apart from give them a drink of water or a cigarette.

This was the reality of war and there wasn't any point brooding about it; there could have been one or two dead in the tunnel, but as far as I was aware no one checked.

We had taken the position and as was usual, once a position was taken we had to move off it quickly; we knew that the ranges on those positions were very precisely known and the enemy knew exactly where to lay their fire down. So it was important to get out of the area as fast as we could. We didn't necessarily have to move too far, just out of the German range.

We then started to comb the rest of the spinney, which was pretty dense in places, for any strays that could be concealed there. At that time we had a Scottish lad with us whose skin was so dark from his time in the desert that he looked more Asiatic than Scottish. He was carrying a Thompson submachine gun and I was walking about 4 yards behind him. We were approaching a bush when suddenly, BANG! He spun round and unloaded the magazine of his machine gun into and around the bush. He then turned to me and said, "Did you no see that? Look at my shoulder." Sure enough a bullet had cut his shoulder strap and burned his tunic. He had wasted no time in emptying that magazine, and the stupid German had paid the price; I call

155

him stupid because he should have realised that in those given circumstances it was futile to stay and fight. The time had come for him to surrender but he had one last very brave show of force, doing his duty, and unfortunately paid for that one 'stupid gesture' with his life.

To me this was a perfect example of how ruthless we had all become; there was more concern shown for this soldier's damaged uniform than for a lost life. War has a terrible effect on a person; if he'd only thrown his gun out and surrendered he would have come to no harm.

It was late afternoon by the time we had taken the spinney and consolidated on the other side of the copse; with the position taken we then sent our prisoners with a suitable escort down to the beaches. Whether or not they made it to the beaches in one piece I don't know; I certainly wouldn't have wanted to go back down the line at that particular moment in time.

We settled down and started to brew ourselves a cup of tea. We each had 48 hour rations consisting of two separate packs containing concentrated tea, sugar and milk. There was also a beef cube, some salt, three bars of chocolate, some boiled sweets and some cigarettes. We also had little tin stoves that contained something like solidified wax for boiling water. You needed two and half hours to boil the bloody water; it was like trying to boil a kettle over a candle.

We lit these things up and eventually I had some very unappetising lukewarm tea and a bar of chocolate. For the next three days my sole intake of food was to be those three bars of chocolate.

I also carried a bar of concentrated chocolate which came in a tin and was like unsweetened solid cocoa. For some reason, after every battle I would have one of these bars of chocolate and then request another, along with a field dressing, as I always seemed to be bandaging someone or other. It got to the stage that as soon as they saw me coming they had the chocolate and dressing ready for me!

I don't think that I could eat the stuff now but I thoroughly enjoyed that chocolate then, and that's what I mainly existed on. Of course with our adrenalin levels running at that rate, food never seemed to be a priority. It was just something that was done to keep us on our feet and we ate purely to keep us going.

After this brief rest we prepared ourselves for a counterattack from the enemy, because we were still in quite an exposed position with very little support, and were expecting an armoured division to pound straight back at us. We had no armour or anti-tank guns so we were ill equipped to deal with an attack if one came either that evening or at first light.

So it was with a certain amount of apprehension that we settled down for our first night on the beachhead.

I noticed that our emotions were very changeable on a day to day basis; some mornings we'd get up feeling very positive ready to take on the day whatever came our way. Then on other days, for no real perceptible reason you would feel like a nervous wreck.

On this day, the 6th June 1944, I personally felt pretty good and content with myself, apart from the obvious loss of life. For me the day had gone very well, and so I settled down in order to try and get some much needed rest before the expected counterattack.

In the early evening we saw our first enemy aircraft, three Focke-Wulfs came flying low over the beaches; they had obviously waited until our fighters had gone back to re-fuel and taken the opportunity in the gathering gloom to make a sortie over the beach-head. These were the first aircraft that we had seen and they took us by surprise; we initially thought that they were our own aircraft and only when they got closer could we see that they were German Focke-Wulfs. They didn't normally pay too much attention to infantrymen, usually looking for a more interesting target. However these were putting on a bit of display just letting us know that the German air force was still there to contend with. It made us think that they would probably pay us another visit at a later date.

We dug in and spent a fairly quiet night with the anticipated counterattack not actually materialising. As soon as we realised there was to be no German attack, we took the opportunity to consolidate our position. Our support came up and the whole battalion formed a line and dug in, we effectively used the breathing space to strengthen our position.

We had lost a large quota of men on the landing so it was up to our brother and sister battalions such as the Durham Light Infantry to cover our backs until we were reinforced. This was how things worked within each battalion; we tended to work as one big unit helping each other out, as and when needed.

We were due to be joined by D-2's, 3's and 4's, providing the landing was a success, which from our point of view it certainly was. We were sitting about seven mile inland holding a line and totally oblivious as to what was going on behind us; it surprised me how ignorant we were to the amount of activity that was going on.

Incidentally the assault troops that landed first on D-Day had a completely different view of it to the one that reporters have subsequently written about.

Looking back now after reading what has been written and seeing photographs and various accounts in newspapers and publications, what has been described by reporters about the D-Day landings seem to have no resemblance to my D-Day. The pictures they portray are completely different from the knowledge of D-Day that is in my head. General Brian Horrocks once said that we belonged to the most exclusive club in the world and on reflection I don't think there can be any better way of describing it.

There were about a dozen reporters on the mother ship with us, but they arrived on the beaches later after the initial assault, and so did not share our experience; we saw those beaches as no one else had. Only those exclusive few had the dubious privilege of witnessing and seeing those beaches as they really were on that morning.

Anyway back to the story. We dug in and our reinforcements arrived, some of whom happened to be old pals, who for one reason or another had been left behind when we set sail.
It was good to meet up with them again and greetings were shared; it was a temporary light hearted break in the grim business of war. We knew that we had a pretty gruesome job before us; as soon as we were reinforced and had sufficient strength we were to push on and extend the beach head, getting it as big and broad as we possibly could in the few remaining hours we had left

No counterattack was forthcoming at this stage which surprised me, because having been in other theatres of war such as the desert; it was my experience to have retaliation from the enemy fairly promptly. This in my opinion was evidence they were caught off guard and how much unprepared they were.

We moved on into the Normandy countryside which was made up of pasture land, cornfields and some heavily wooded country; this was interspersed with various farm buildings. We still had our tanks with us and we worked on the basis of two sections up and one in reserve. Each section would have a turn at being up front before then moving to the rear for someone else to become point section. It was a nerve wracking job, because as section leader I had to be out front, when it was our turn to be point section. In close country you were not aware of any trouble until it happened and you were actually fired on. This was where the nerves really took a hammering; all senses were heightened as we anticipated being attacked and having to take evasive action.

Although I was a full corporal I never actually wore the sign of my rank during any of the operations that I took part in. This was understood by the whole platoon, possibly the whole company. I always contended that the only people concerned with my rank were my compatriots and they all knew me.

To my mind it wasn't just a question of holding that rank, but having the knowledge and experience which went with it. I had grown up in the reality of war and now I was an expert, a veteran. I had earned the respect of the other men and even those who were years my senior would never question any decision that I made. My experience had taught me what to expect; my ears had become so tuned-in to the various sounds, that I knew when I heard mortar bombs going off, exactly where and when they were likely to land. It's things like this that gives you the true rank and authority.

I carried my stripes in my haversack; I always thought that if there was a sniper sitting up a tree looking for a target then the first to be picked was likely to be the platoon commander, the second lieutenant or the C.O. if he could get a bang at him. Failing that he would target the lesser officers, then the platoon sergeant and then the first N.C.O. he could pinpoint. Only when he was really pushed would he get down to the 'odds and sods' and I preferred to be in that category.

So far it had worked out pretty well for me but we had lost quite a lot of officers and I believe this was because they were recognisable as such. Personally I think this was a mistake because we all knew our officers; we didn't need a polished pip to recognise authority in the middle of a battle and we knew them all by their Christian names.

Moving forward I was in point section twice; we considered it a rest when it was our turn to move to the rear and let someone else take the lead. We did this for two days with very little opposition to speak of; although the counterattack hadn't come it was obvious that things were building up. Defences were being thrown up in front of us but as yet we hadn't hit the real core of any organised resistance. We probed the countryside and we knew sooner or later we were going to bump it. On the morning of D-4 we were on a country lane that led to a farmhouse and we had a company on each side of the road; there were two sections up and on this occasion I was bringing up the rear, a very fortunate position to be in as events were soon to prove.

There were tall trees and very close hedging bordering the lane which led to the farm buildings; once past the hedge we went through an old farm building, crossed over a ditch and into a cornfield. At the end of the cornfield there was a pasture field and on the far side of that a farmhouse standing just off the road.

The first two sections made their way into the pasture field; they had just got about half way between the edge of the corn and the farmhouse, when suddenly the farmhouse erupted with a hail of machine gun fire. They had no option but to try and rush the farmhouse because we were pinned down in the cornfield from sniper fire to our rear.

163

We had walked into a first class ambush and were paying the price; we really were in a right pickle. I made a quick assessment of where things were positioned and dropped into the corn, then immediately crawled on my stomach to about three yards from my drop point. I decided to head for the track to get to the farmhouse from the rear.

Obviously I couldn't see anyone else and they didn't know where I was, and so the only contact we had was verbal. I called each member of the section name by name to let them know my position, and tried to arrange everyone to head in the same direction. While this was going on the sniper was still trying to pick us out of the cornfield and I was crawling along trying not to disturb the top of the corn to give my position away.

The sniper who was trying to nail me came pretty close to his mark on a couple of occasions as I heard the crack of the bullets as they passed my ear. I was very much aware that when you heard that crack, they were far too close for comfort.

I was halfway through the cornfield when somebody grabbed my ankles; it was someone in my section that I'd had bother with previously because of his nervous disposition. He didn't seem as if he was going to let go of my ankles and I almost had to kick him in the face to get him to release me. He was an ex-paratrooper but why he was

164

with us nobody knew; I didn't even think he should have been there at all. But thinking about it now, it would be extremely unkind to blame anyone for showing fear in those circumstances. However, I finally managed to persuade him to let go and instructed him to follow me to the track.

There was an officer in the cornfield and he kept shouting, checking on my whereabouts and asking me if I could see anything. Jokingly I said "Why don't you pop your head up and have a look?" Well he must have actually popped his head up and someone took a shot at him, because all we could hear was him swearing his head off, with all of his composure gone!

I managed to get the whole section out of the cornfield and onto the track, or rather I thought it was the whole section, but we then realised that someone was missing. It was one of my old friends and we tried calling him, but it looked like I was going to have to go back in to search for him. The others were saying "Leave the bugger there", but we all knew that wasn't really an option.

The tanks were trundling along the track firing into the treetops and so that put paid to any more sniper fire. I was just crossing the ditch ready to enter the corn when this chap appeared on the track coming towards us. It turned out that he hadn't even been in the cornfield. He was at the rear of the section and when he saw the first two sections being bombarded with heavy machine gun fire he had decided that it would be better to not go into the cornfield at all. Instead he hopped behind a wall to sit it out, which I suppose if you're not looking for medals, is as good a thing to do as anything.

I rallied the section together and we moved on up the track. The transport was there and the stretcher bearers were already in the pasture field doing their work. We were able to go straight through, because the farmhouse had already been taken from the rear, by the company that was on the other side of the road to us along with the tanks.

By this time the Germans had taken off, but not before cutting our first two sections to absolute ribbons. The Germans still had firepower directed onto the area around the farmhouse and so on retiring they had to pass through their own fire

The thing that impressed me most on that particular morning was our Padre, who I had last seen in Boscombe with his wife. On that occasion he was pushing a pram around the town, greeting everyone he met like a typical village vicar. At that time Boscombe was absolutely overflowing with troops. We were no angels and I'm afraid the Padre only ever saw us when we were compulsorily sent to church.

This morning I saw a completely different Padre working under fire; he was there in his shirt sleeves still wearing his dog collar, running in and out of the cornfield bringing out our wounded. I don't know if they decorate Padres but this little chap certainly deserved to receive some recognition for his bravery on that day. I felt that it was our job and he didn't have to be there. His actions that day impressed me greatly; I was of the strong opinion that one shouldn't be critical of a person that didn't appear to be tough, because behind that dog collar there was an awful lot of man.

We continued up the track and once past the farmhouse we were on our own again. I was leading one section and we were joined by another that was being led by an old pal of mine, Ginger Leonard from Manchester. We had been through the desert campaign together and it was good to see him again. We made our way to the far end of the farmyard which led out into open country with a forest on the hill beyond.

There was some enemy fire coming from the trees, and so we gathered together to discuss plans for tackling the copse. While we were talking, and before we had a chance to launch an attack, low and behold to our complete surprise, the Germans began to come out of the copse with their hands up!

Perhaps they'd had enough and wanted to surrender before our attack began. There were about six or seven of them and they were pretty bedraggled. They were obviously quite soused up from drinking the cider that every farm seemed to have. Ginger kept them covered and I got them to put their hands on their heads and relieved them of their weapons, making them safe to send back down the line.

We made the decision to send two sections forward into the copse, and although we didn't relish the prospect, thought it had to be done to ensure that the position was properly taken.

Just then the C.O. appeared looking a bit of a shambles in my opinion, with his valise hanging half way down his back and hardly recognisable as a soldier. He was carrying a walking stick which was something all officers did for some reason. "What are you going to do Corporal?" he asked. I informed him of our plans and he replied, "Don't go any further, I want you to stay here and cover our withdrawal". I was somewhat taken aback, "Withdrawal?" I was thinking it seemed a bit odd as the Germans were offering themselves up and we were pulling out.

He could see my surprise and explained that we had to get out of there because there was a lot of German armour coming round on our right, and we had no means of stopping it. We had already been caught out earlier in the day and lost a lot of men; with heavy armour coming we would have been slaughtered.

I arranged with Ginger for his section to go first, then after a couple of minutes I would follow on and then go through his section; this was usually the way we worked.

The copse was still being fired on and in fact there was rather a lot of lead flying about. Not really a healthy place to be upon reflection. One of my lads had positioned himself behind a big chestnut tree with a trunk that must have been a yard across. It was a pretty safe place to be and I think he would have been happy to have stayed there but one cannot fight a war from behind a chestnut tree! We got him out and back onto the track where we eventually managed to get into a position to march down the lane with a fair degree of safety.

As we passed by the farmhouse we could see all of our dead casualties lying by the side of the road; it was a heart rending sight. I knew them all and found myself becoming terrified to look, wondering who I would see next.

It was one of those moments that could play on your mind and stop you from being able to sleep at night. A person cannot cope with the horror, and it has to be put somewhere in the back of one's mind, where it would stay unless you consciously brought it to the fore.

I always thought that seeing such horrors would cause me to lose sleep, however I had become very good at compartmentalising my thoughts.

We were due to meet up with our transport who were laying on a meal for us at a point in an orchard about two miles further on. What was left of the company was a truly pitiful sight; we had really taken a beating. Out of the company which would normally consist of between 150 and 200 men, we would have struggled to raise a platoon of between 30 to 50 men.

As we broke out from the close country and into the orchard the sun was shining and it was a beautiful June evening, but not where we wanted to be. Our company cooks were standing by our trucks with their dixies (cooking pots) ready with a hot meal in the hope of cheering us up. Each person went along the line and as the cook was dishing out the grub he was enquiring after various people; trying to find out if friends or possibly relatives had made it. My turn came and he asked me how many more were coming. I told him that we were the last section, and there were only five of us. "Are there no more behind you?" he asked. When I told him that we were the last, he began to cry, but continued serving food with tears streaming down his face.

There was nothing more to be said. This was how we all felt and we separated into groups sitting down in silence to eat our food. There really was nothing to say; it had all been said back at the farmhouse, and now we were all feeling very down and more than a bit depressed.

With time to reflect I told myself that was another battle behind us, but I also began to wonder how much more of this could a person endure?

Suddenly I felt a pat on my shoulder and on turning round I saw that it was my old pal Rennie. I wasn't sure whether to be pleased to see him or annoyed that he was there. If anyone had asked who I would like to see again at that moment, then Rennie would have been the first person that I would have thought of. However, I didn't like the fact that he once again was in the thick of it. Initially I gave him a bit of a dressing down. "What the hell are you doing here? Have you no sense, volunteering to get back to this?" Nonetheless it was really good to have him with me at that moment in time and we settled down to chat. He wanted to know about everything that I'd been through since we last saw each other. I said "Well you know Rennie, day by day it's getting worse. We're only just beginning to 'bump the opposition' and they haven't even got warmed up yet, so goodness knows what the future holds for us."

Once again Rennie was unfazed as he had so much confidence in my decisions, and he was of the opinion that as long as I was there, then everything would be alright.

171

I was no expert, just knowledgeable from having gained a lot of experience, so this made me cross. He felt that as long as we were together we'd be ok, but that put an awful lot of pressure on me.

We were always talking if we got a spare moment about what we intended doing when the war was over. Rennie wanted us to go into business together. He wanted us to get a farm, with me working on the building side of things, and him looking after the cows. Which was just as well because what I knew about cows was what came on my Sunday dinner plate! We were planning for the future and were fighting in a war, and for an ideal that we believed in, and we thought God willing, after it was over that we would get what we deserved, or the chance that we felt we deserved. We were really going to make a go of this partnership; we had it all worked out, but like a lot of well laid schemes, they don't always work out as planned.

Once again we received reinforcements and moved up into the close countryside. I think it would have been the 15th or 16th June and I wasn't to know it, but my time on the beachhead in Normandy was running out. In fact it was a lot closer than ever I could have imagined.

Moving forward we alternated from point section, to rear section, and so on. The mood had changed and everyone seemed to be a bit edgy. It was proving to be more and more difficult to instil a light-hearted attitude into the section. Which by now was composed mainly of new lads; some of them hadn't been tried out at all. It was my job to try and reassure those lads that they had nothing to worry about, but that was an impossible task in the position we were in.

On the morning of the 17th June we were laying in a position to the west of Tilly-sur-Seulles in very close country. I was in a pasture field near to a farmhouse and I wasn't very happy about it because my field of fire was negligible. We had a new company commander that I hadn't met before and he had placed my section in this pasture field, which didn't sit very easily with me. We were under persistent sniper fire and one lad had already been shot in the ankle. I was raising quite a stink about being so exposed and sent word to the company commander that I wanted the position changed, but he didn't leave his position to come and check on us. I was by now getting very angry when a major happened to come along. He was well known to me and asked what was wrong. "Well just look at where we are, sitting in the middle of this open field." I said to him. He replied "Corporal, you put your men where you think they will be most effective, and I will clear it with the lieutenant in charge of the platoon." I therefore moved the section from the centre of the pasture field to the edge of the track that led down to the farmhouse.

The track was made up of well packed cobbles, with a small embankment measuring about eighteen inches to the side; we decided that we would dig in alongside the embankment. We mounted the gun on the other side of the embankment because this was a fairly good defence position, and it allowed us to cover the immediate fields adjacent to the farmhouse. The officer still didn't come over to review the position, and to be honest I was feeling pretty worked up about it.

I then placed the men as I saw fit. We only had one pick and shovel between us in order to dig ourselves in. I decided to let the lads use them first, while I to the best of my ability scooped out a shallow slit trench at the foot of the small embankment. It was as hard as the hobs of hell and I only managed to get about six inches below the surface. When the lads were all finished with the pick and shovel I intended to get myself well down and dug in before nightfall. Above in a cloudless sky there were two Typhoons patrolling over our heads and as long as they were there I felt sure that no one would try any hanky panky. They would be on the lookout for any gun flashes or mortar fire and were equipped with bombs and rockets. It should be noted that the Typhoons were a very successful ground-attack aircraft. No one with any sense would open fire whilst they were up there, so I was feeling reasonably safe for the moment. It was now late in the day but earlier on I had been feeling pretty nervous and on edge. We all had days like that but I simply told myself that it was all in my head. I then settled down to have my evening meal thinking nothing was going to happen at this late stage in the day.

Rennie was in another section but he turned up with a sultana pudding for me; it was really just an excuse for a bit of a chat before we finally dug in for the night. I ate my pudding and before settling down I had to go and get the orders for the following day's operations. It was to be more of the same probe, probe, probe, until we bumped into trouble, and we knew sooner or later that we'd bump it.
After receiving our orders I had a brief word with the new lieutenant who didn't seem particularly pleased with me, but I was happy with the position that we'd taken up; fateful though that later proved to be.

I gave the lads our orders, put Lee on the gun as lookout and the rest were busy digging in. I was sitting on the embankment waiting until I could get the shovel, kicking at the hole with my feet but not getting anywhere fast. The ground was so hard that our entrenching tools were of no use whatsoever, and so there was really no alternative but to wait.

As I was sitting there I heard the POP, POP, POP POP of the mortars and I turned to Lee and said, "Take cover there's some mortars coming over". I dropped into my slit trench which as yet was not very deep and looked up.

The Typhoons were already diving to the gun flashes that they'd seen on the ground. As I looked up and the Typhoons hit, I said to myself "Well they're going to have 'tubs to mend' when those Typhoons hit them."

That Fateful Day

When the first bomb dropped it was too close; I knew when it dropped it was almost on top of us and I just had time to think, "Good gracious this is it". The next one blew me up in the air and I didn't know what hit me.

The whole world seemed to burst and the noise in my head was absolutely terrific. It is hard to describe but it was like being in a swimming baths that was so full of screaming children that you dive under the water to get away from the sound. But when you resurface the noise is absolutely overwhelming. The whole world seemed to be revolving round and round; everything was spinning and I thought "Good God I'm dying."

As the mortar bombs came in salvos of six, there was still four more landing around us. The embankment had gone, and I was on my knees on top of the area that used to be the embankment. My left arm was flying about uncontrollably; it was above my head and I had to grab it with my other hand. I was thinking "Good gracious, it's been severed at the shoulder."
I still had this intense noise in my head and was trying to get to my feet but everything was swimming about. The horizon was swaying as if I was on a boat. All I could think about was, "Oh God, I've lost an arm; an arm, an arm, oh no!

The lads in the section ran to me and helped me to my feet; they patted my body saying "You're alright, you're alright, there's not a mark on you." "It's my arm" I said, and as soon as I let go, the arm jumped sky high; it seemed to have a life of its own. I had to grab it again; but they still couldn't see anything wrong, and told me that it must be shock. My legs were like jelly and I was feeling extremely worried; I had one lad on either side of me and one behind, trying to help me up the track. I was still wearing my tin hat and they were all talking to me, trying to reassure me that I was okay; I was convinced that they were lying to me.

Suddenly their attitude changed when they looked at me again and they said, "Good God!" Then I felt the hot blood running down my face.

I had been hit in the head by something which had pierced through my tin hat and gone into my skull. I always wore my hat pretty firmly on my head with the chin strap well done up. The rubber headpiece inside must have been acting like a seal. When the tin hat filled with blood it lifted and then all of the blood inside came gushing out!

The sight of this must have been appalling for the lads, because about half a pail full of blood had gushed out all at once, and I was absolutely drenched. Their faces couldn't hide how shocked they were. "Oh good heavens" I heard them say.

It was my good fortune that day to be only yards from our medical officer; God had arranged my wound that day.

From where I was wounded I only had to get about thirty yards to the medical officer and an ambulance. I managed to walk nine tenths of the way before my legs gave way; the lads dragged me the rest of the way.

The medical officer removed my tin hat and immediately tried to stop the bleeding; he then gave me a shot of morphine.

By this time I was unable to speak coherently; I was feeling incredibly weak from the enormous blood loss, and was going in and out of consciousness. It was somewhat disconcerting to see the lads looking at me shaking their heads; an officer I knew came over and when he saw me just said, "Oh no, I don't believe it." He went away and I was left thinking that I must look pretty bad, as no one was making any attempt to talk to me.

I didn't see Rennie again; the last time I saw him was when he had brought me that sultana pudding.

It must have seemed odd at the time, but I suddenly thought about my haversack; it contained a clean change of underwear, socks and all the basics needed for the life we were living. I thought it would be a waste just to leave it on the ground, so I told the lads to take it.

After receiving emergency treatment I was whisked into an ambulance and off I went. I passed through from one aid post to another, getting checked at each one.

Bits of my hair had been clipped off; the vest that I was wearing had been lily-white, but now the whole thing had been dyed a perfect blood red. There wasn't one patch of white remaining, not one patch. The amount of blood that I had lost must have been terrific.

That was my exit from combat; I didn't know it then, but the war was over for me. I cannot help to this day marvelling at the set-up which permitted me to live and walk away from such an experience.

Finally I arrived at the field hospital which had been set up on the beachhead; such hospitals are under canvas, like large marquees. Here emergency treatment was provided along with some operations; if anything more complicated arrived they would evacuate them to a base hospital that was better equipped. I wasn't taken straight into the hospital, but remained in the ambulance for what seemed a very long time.

I think my concept of time was affected by my injury and the fact that I was dropping in and out of consciousness. At one stage a nursing sister did come in to check on me. While I lay there in the ambulance I could hear all the gun fire and I felt pretty exposed in that position. Being an infantryman I would have been much happier lying on the ground.

I lay there until the following morning when I was taken into the hospital; the doctor in charge looked at me then sent me back to the ambulance. I enquired as to where I was going and was told that I was going down to the harbour to be taken home.

I knew nothing about the Mulberry Harbour at this time; the last I'd heard it mentioned it was still on paper in the planning stage. They intended to ship me back to England to be operated on, but we arrived at the harbour to learn that no shipping was leaving the harbour because of the atrocious weather. I later learned that one harbour had been destroyed, and the other one which I was to depart from was damaged and couldn't be used. I had a very bumpy ride back to the field hospital, and by this time my wound was quite painful. Prior to that, I hadn't really felt it.

On my arrival back at the hospital I was given some soup then once more taken back to the ambulance. This time they informed me that I was going to be flown out. So bump, bump, bump, off we went again; all I was conscious of was the inside of the ambulance and the motion as we travelled along the bumpy road. We got to the airfield and were there for quite a while, before then for some reason we headed back to the field hospital.

I was placed on the floor of the hospital where I stayed for about fifteen minutes; I was then approached by a doctor who was either American or Canadian. I wasn't sure which, but he spoke with an accent in what I would describe as 'Colonial English', if I can put it like that. He began to explain to me what was about to happen. "We're going to do a little job on you today, I'm going to put this needle in your arm, and don't worry it will be a very nice experience." I was surprised that nothing seemed to be happening; I didn't have the pleasing happy feeling I expected and didn't feel drowsy.

They moved me into the operating theatre where I could see all of the nurses masked and gowned up at the ready. They lifted me onto the table and at this point I was thinking "Things are getting a bit out of hand here, I'd better tell someone how I'm feeling." I thought by this time I should be completely unconscious but they started clipping a sheet over my head. So I said to them, "Before you start, I know exactly what you are doing and I'm conscious of everything that's going on." They smiled and told me to relax and not to worry; everything was as it should be. They put something on my ankles possibly straps; it felt like a cold water bandage. I was paralysed on my left side from the waist up and my arm had to be strapped down, as it was still flailing about.

The next thing I knew was 'zip, zip, zip', and I could actually feel him cutting through my scalp; he cut what I would describe as an Isle of Man type three legged pattern away from the wound. He folded the points back towards my neck; I was still conscious and once again I reminded him that I was still very much aware of everything, and once again he told me not to worry.

He then proceeded to break the bone around the wound; apparently this needed to be done in order to pick the pieces of shrapnel out. I could hear the shrapnel being dropped into a metal dish; after that he took a drill or some sort of sanding machine, and proceeded to smooth the area around the hole and over the top of my scalp.

It was a remarkable thing to experience, because I was fully aware of everything that was happening, but there was no sensation of pain. Then the wound was stitched and it was time for the nurses to bandage my head. I was looking at them but by this time everything was out of focus. My head was bandaged in Plaster of Paris and at this point I became totally relaxed, and realising that it was all over fell asleep.

The next thing that I knew I was back in the ambulance; the surgeon came to check me over and asked how I was. When I told him that I felt fine he said I would be home shortly because I was to be flown out.

As promised I was flown from the beachhead in a Dakota with a lot of walking wounded; I was the only stretcher case and was placed on the floor of the plane. The others were standing or sitting around me.

There was an R.A.F. stewardess in charge and she was going round handing out boiled sweets and cigarettes to the lads; she looked at me but passed me by. "Are there no sweets for me?" I asked. She apologised and explained she didn't think that I would be capable of eating them, but I hadn't had anything to eat in ages. I think I could have eaten the plane! So I got my sweets and she sat down next to me to keep me company; she was a nice girl. There was nothing to see from the plane's window unless we were banking over, then I got a glimpse of the horizon.

I was wounded on the evening of the 17th June and think it was late at night on the 21st June when I landed in England. Four R.A.F. lads carried me into a hangar and set me down on the floor. A Padre came round to get our details in order to send field messages off to our various next of kin, to let them know how we were. People were fussing about trying to sort out where we were all heading. We had landed in Abingdon and I was bound for Oxford, which wasn't too far away.

We were given a meal and a cup of tea and after a while I was put in an ambulance bound for Oxford. It was about 1.00 am by this time and I was joined in the ambulance by a

W.A.A.F. I was very surprised to discover that she was the very same W.A.A.F. that had left the beachhead with me. It had been daytime when we left and so she had been on duty for a very long time. Presumably she must have been detailed to accompany me right to the hospital in Oxford.

I was delivered to the hospital where there were a couple of porters and a nursing sister on duty. They put me to bed where I stayed undisturbed till morning.

The following day I was visited by a neurologist who spent about two hours asking me all sorts of questions; he wanted to know where I'd been and what I'd done. He asked about the beachhead, what unit I was in and what I had been doing leading up to the time that I was wounded. Basically he was testing my memory and brain function, and he recorded everything in his notebook.

He was back again the following two mornings with similar questions; he also gave me various things to taste like sugar or mustard and salt, and also things to test my sense of smell such as vinegar. Everything was written down in his notes. The nursing staff would check me on a regular basis; they would take my temperature and ask how I was doing. Of course they couldn't check the wound as I still had my plaster hat on.

My stay in hospital proved to be uneventful; there was no backward slip. I continued to make good progress with no complications at all; it was just a question of time before they could take the lid off my head!

There is a story that I found rather touching. Before I left the beachhead there was a Major Small, a surgeon whose wife was a sister at the hospital that I was sent to in Oxford. Before I left the beachhead he'd written a letter to his wife on my plaster cast; when the nurses saw it they went running off to find this sister so she could read the letter from her husband. I thought this was something really special; every so often others would turn up just to read the letter! I never did find out what happened to my plaster cap once they had removed it. Perhaps she kept it? It would certainly have made a unique souvenir!
The surgeon did a pretty good job that day under very stressful conditions; I haven't experienced any ill effects from the wound since the surgery, and have nothing but admiration for that major. I would be happy for him to operate on me anytime.

On my first day out of bed I had to go to the dining room; on the way I met one of the lads from the company. He was as surprised to see me as I was to see him; his first greeting was "Pity about Rennie."

Of course I'd been completely out of touch with everything that had been going on. It turned out that poor Rennie had been killed in action not long after I was wounded. He was caught in machine gunfire and that was the end of my pal Rennie. I was absolutely devastated and subsequently lost all interest in what was happening with the war.

I knew that I was now physically incapable of going back to the war; I'd done the job that was required of me. There was now a long hard road to get back to some sort of normality; something which I found particularly hard. I never saw any of the lads from the platoon or company again; some quite possibly thought I was dead.

That was the end of my war; from then on it was a case of doing barrack room duties until the day I was discharged.

When I look back at the circumstances surrounding the time of my wounding, I realise how fortunate I was. If it had happened earlier in the day I wouldn't have survived; when I was hit, I was so close to the Regimental Aid Post where I received immediate emergency treatment. I was losing so much blood and certainly couldn't afford to lose any more, and so on reflection I consider myself very lucky to have walked away from it.

I believe that there is a reason that I survived that day and that I had a special purpose in life; others will have to make their own judgement.

Seasons in the Sun

Goodbye to you my trusted friend
We've known each other since we were nine or ten
Together we've climbed hills and trees
Learned of love and ABC's
Skinned our hearts and skinned our knees
Goodbye my friend it's hard to die
When all the birds are singing in the sky
Now that spring is in the air
Pretty girls are everywhere
Think of me and I'll be there
We had joy, we had fun
We had seasons in the sun
But the hills that we climbed
Were just seasons out of time
Goodbye Papa please pray for me
I was the black sheep of the family
You tried to teach me right from wrong
Too much wine and too much song
Wonder how I got along
Goodbye Papa it's hard to die
When all the birds are singing in the sky
Now that the spring is in the air
Little children everywhere.

NB: My father played this song at the end of his Recordings.
(Sung by Andy Williams.)

Addendum

After Combat

My father made a good recovery from his wounds and was sent to Scotland to Camp 293, Camp Carronbridge, Thornhill, Dumfries, which was a prisoner of war camp. There he was tasked with guarding the German prisoners of war.

Originally Carronbridge was used by the Norwegians and later for training allied troops. In 1945 it was turned into P.O.W. Camp 293 and both prisoners and the troops in charge were housed in Nissan huts.

Picture of a Nissan hut at Carronbridge
(Taken from the Canmore site

190

The German prisoners produced a camp magazine called 'Unsere Welt' (Our World) during their internment.

A special edition of the camp magazine was produced in 1947 for a sports day. It was written in German and English and contained articles about their lives in the camp and sport.

Picture from Catawiki.com.

My father built good relationships with many of the internees and he used to tell me stories about how he would ask them to sing their German marching songs because he loved hearing them. This was apparently against the rules, but it seemed that my father didn't always follow the rules!

There was one prisoner in particular with whom my father had built a good rapport. His name was Adolph Küchel and he was an extremely talented artist. He painted two portraits for my father, one of him and one of my mother. The latter was copied from a photograph that my father carried with him, and both portraits captured their likeness perfectly. These paintings always took pride of place on the walls of my childhood home and subsequently in my own adult home.

I tried periodically over the years to find any information about this artist, including contacting the German Embassy and the Consulate in Edinburgh but to no avail.
Then in 2021 I was looking online at pages from the camp magazine 'Unsere Welt' and in one of the pages Adolph Küchel was credited with doing some of the sketches for the magazine.

Next to this someone had written that he had remained
in Scotland in Moniaive, married and had a son.
I was overjoyed and began searching the area online.

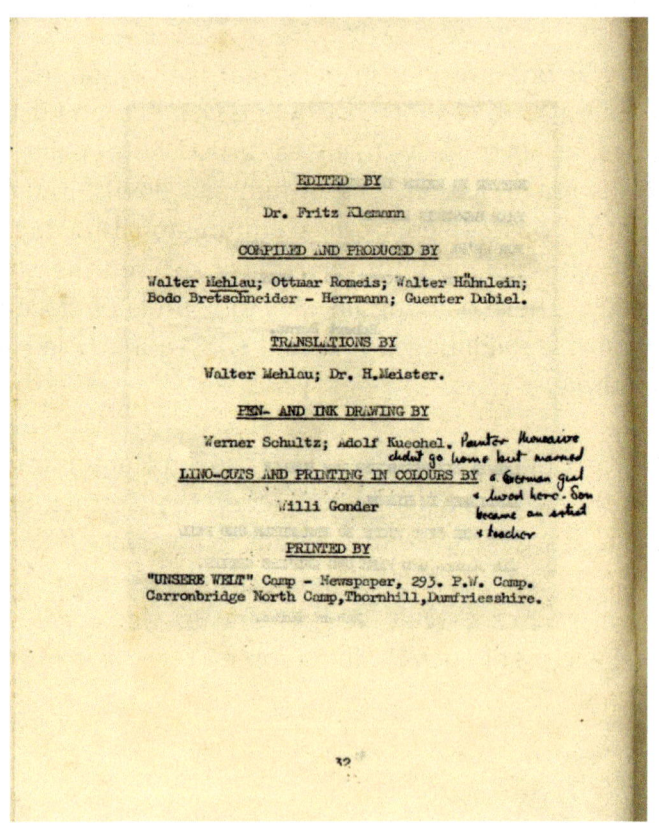

EDITED BY

Dr. Fritz Klemann

COMPILED AND PRODUCED BY

Walter Mehlau; Ottmar Romeis; Walter Hähnlein;
Bodo Bretschneider - Herrmann; Guenter Dubiel.

TRANSLATIONS BY

Walter Mehlau; Dr. H.Meister.

PEN- AND INK DRAWING BY

Werner Schultz; Adolf Kuechel. *Painter Moniaive*
didnt go home but married
LINO-CUTS AND PRINTING IN COLOURS BY *a German girl*
+ lived here. Son
Willi Gonder *became an artist*
+ teacher

PRINTED BY

"UNSERE WELT" Camp - Newspaper, 293. P.W. Camp.
Carronbridge North Camp,Thornhill,Dumfriesshire.

193

I managed to find a Facebook site for Glencairn Community Council, Moniaive, Dumfries and Galloway, and sent a message asking for any information on Adolph's son. Very quickly I received a response from a lady in charge of the site. Amazingly she had actually met him and felt sure that she could find some contact details.

Very soon I had his address and was able to write and send him photos of the two portraits painted by his father all of those years ago. This was a revelation to him as he had no knowledge of the artwork done by his father during his time in the camp.

My father was discharged from the Green Howards on the 27th March 1946 and settled into civilian life. I am eternally grateful that he recorded his wartime memoirs for his family to keep and treasure.

I first started this project almost 20 years ago after I discovered my father's tape recordings. At first I was unable to listen to them because I found it all too emotional.

However, I eventually began the laborious task of typing them up. I wanted to transcribe them myself, in order to try and retain the character of the man, and hopefully I have succeeded in doing that.

In many ways it has been a labour of love and although at times things in life have got in the way, I have never given up on the idea of writing up his memoirs. As I said in my introduction, I have tried to faithfully transcribe my father's own spoken words into this book.

Jan King (Blackburn) July 2022

Painting of my father by Adolf Küchel.

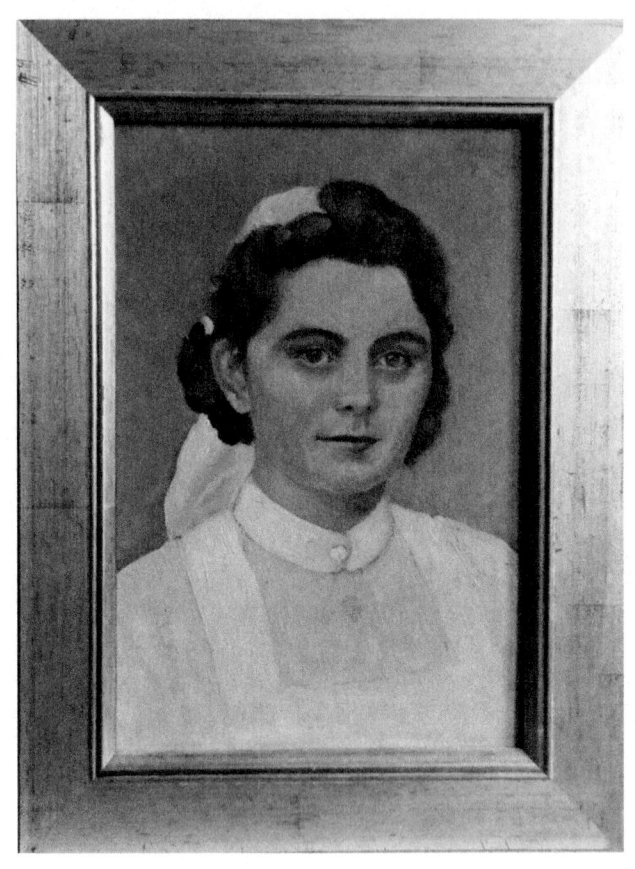

Painting of my mother.

Printed in Great Britain
by Amazon

63273271R00117